ANYONE CAN BE
PRESIDENT

The Super-Smart Guide to
Being the Ruler of the Free World

DAVID VIENNA

KNOCK
KNOCK®
LOS ANGELES, CALIFORNIA

Created, published, and distributed by Knock Knock
6080 Center Drive
Los Angeles, CA 90045
knockknockstuff.com
Knock Knock is a registered trademark of Knock Knock LLC

Illustrations by Peter Strain

Images used under license from Shutterstock.com:
7: AP; 8: wantanddo; 9: George R. Skadding / AP; 10: Jack
Fordyce; 13: Nara Archives; BJ / AP; 23: Universal History
Archive / Universal Images Group; 23: Universal History Archive;
24: Greg Smith / AP; 24: The Art Archive; 29: Underwood
Archives / UIG; 30: Jeff Chiu / AP; 36: Marion Curtis / StarPix; 36:
catwalker; 50: spatuletail; 50: Everett Historical; 57: Rena Schild;
60:JStone; 77: Harvey Georges / AP; 78: Gilbert Stuart / Everett
Art; 85: Everett Historical; 88: Georgios Kollidas; 90: Everett
Historical; 91: Michael Reynolds / EPA-EFE; 99: Lederhandler
/ AP; 101: Universal History Archive / Universal Images Group;
101: Gilbert Stuart / Everett Art; 101: Everett Historical; 102:
Unknown; 102: John Kropewnicki; 102: Frank L Junior; 104: AP;
106: Brendan Howard; 106: Henry Griffin / AP; 115: AP; Back
Cover: Georgios Kollidas

ISBN: 978-168349111-8
UPC: 825703503005

10 9 8 7 6 5 4 3 2 1

Dedicated to the American voter,
who gets us into and out of almost
every problem our country faces.

TABLE OF CONTENTS

INTRODUCTION

In the United States we tell our children they can be anything they want to when they grow up, often adding the coda "even president!" That's because our government is truly one "of the people, by the people, for the people." Some guy named Abraham Lincoln said that in a famous speech. Of course, he borrowed the phrase from some other dude named John Wycliffe and failed to credit him for it, thus continuing a long-standing tradition of politicians taking undue credit for stuff (but I digress...).

Yes, literally any naturally born American citizen over the age of thirty-five who has lived in the country for fourteen consecutive years can be president. That's it. Those are the only legal requirements. You don't need a college degree or a clean record or even clean underwear.

But really, we all know there's more to it than that. So, what does it truly take to become the ruler of the free world?

Anyone Can Be President is here to answer that question with a like, totally erudite, super thorough completely nonpartisan examination of what it takes to sit in the Oval Office (in the big important chair, not on the couch). We'll look at historical trends as well as the habits of previous presidents; proffer tons of graphs, quizzes, charts, surveys other super serious stuff. This semi-practical, semi-interactive tome is the seminal guide to everything any (and we do mean any!) actual or accidental aspiring candidate or mildly curious citizen needs to know about landing in the highest office in the land—from the required mental health test and presidential fashion tips to sample scenarios for you to tackle while you're staring at that big ol' nuclear launch button on your desk. (Think: *Schoolhouse Rock* for "adults," minus the music. And the animation. And the 1970s cred.)

Upon completion of this book, you should not only have a basic comprehension of how to be president, but also a bunch of tools to help you secure the gig. And we really need you to run. Yes, YOU. The need is sizable. You might say it's bigly.

CHAPTER 1

CAN YOU (REALLY) BE PRESIDENT?

ELIGIBILITY

OFFICIAL (AND UNOFFICIAL) REQUIREMENTS

There are only three official requirements for anyone who wants to run for president. If you're learning this for the first time, that means you must've skipped the introduction, which means you like to leap headlong into situations without first doing the required studying and therefore might make an excellent president. But you're not president yet, so let's go over them.

According to Article 2, Section 1, of the U.S. Constitution (and no, that's not a Starfleet ship), anyone who seeks the position of president must:

★ BE A NATURAL-BORN CITIZEN OF THE UNITED STATES

★ HAVE LIVED IN SAID UNITED STATES FOR 14 CONSECUTIVE YEARS

★ BE AT LEAST 35 YEARS OF AGE

So, chances are if you like bacon-cheddar dogs but can't enjoy them because of your cholesterol, you meet all three of these requirements.

But wait, as they say in late-night infomercials, there's more.

Even the most misinformed student knows a president can serve a maximum of eight years and each term is four years. But as late as the mid-twentieth century, a president could hold office longer than that. The term limit was largely a traditional gesture that honored good ol' George Washington, who refused to run for a third term way back in 1796. He figured we'd just split from a monarchy, and there was no need to start that mess up again. But as happens often in politics, eventually someone broke with tradition.

"RULES ARE NOT NECESSARILY SACRED, PRINCIPLES ARE."

—PRESIDENT FRANKLIN D. ROOSEVELT

After two fruitful terms as president, Franklin D. Roosevelt decided to give tradition the finger and run for another term or two. And he won. Yes, FDR was elected four times and is the only president to serve more than eight years. He may have attempted to go for another term, but he decided to die instead.

So, Congress (we'll get into what that is later in the book) saw that anyone could pull the same move and put forth an amendment to the Constitution in 1947 that would limit the number of terms a person could serve. That way they wouldn't have to rely on divine intervention to keep one person from remaining in power for too long. That was ratified by the states, which basically means they had to go "Meh…okay," and thus the 22nd Amendment became legit law in 1951.

Official eligibility may be summed up in three bullet points, but the innumerable unofficial requirements for being prez are pretty much bonkers. Statistically, it helps if you're an old, rich, white dude. As of the writing of this book, forty-four out of forty-five presidents have been pasty geezers. To be clear, this is purely statistical. Being an old, rich, white dude does not guarantee you'll be good at the job. Quite the contrary, based on the track record of a great number of previous presidents who qualified as such.

Theodore Roosevelt was a boyish 42 years old when he took office. #youngestprezever

If you have the gift of gab, as they say, that will definitely work in your favor. After all, when your audience is the entire population of the world, people tend to pay attention to what you say and how you say it. So, if you need your "ask not what your country can do for you" or "four score and seven years ago" moment, you should go get yourself a dictionary, a thesaurus, and a whole lot of scratch paper. (Of course, being able to actually read and write is not a requirement.) But enough of this wordy claptrap. Let's get started on the practical stuff.

MENTAL HEALTH TEST

Every once in a while, a candidate's sanity comes into question. Of course, this always seems to happen after they've taken office.

No one needed to worry about Rutherford B. Hayes's mental acuity. He worried about it enough himself. Reportedly, Hayes, a staunch abolitionist and our nineteenth president, suffered from lyssophobia, which is the fear of going insane. Surely, the fact that worrying about something too much can make you go mad was not lost on him.

Some people on Capitol Hill and beyond worried about Ronald Reagan's mental state after a few public gaffes and blank stares.

Donald Trump took an actual test for mental fitness after politicians, the press, and the public voiced concern about his erratic behavior. Trump's test reportedly involved identifying simple images, so that's what we're going to do right now. Because we can all agree that whoever is running things over at the White House should, at the very least, be able to see a picture of a traffic cone and say, "That's a traffic cone."

Oh, and if you do plan to run for president, do not share your results or the fact that you've even taken this test. While we want our leaders to be mentally fit, we don't want to know they had to be tested to prove that is the case.

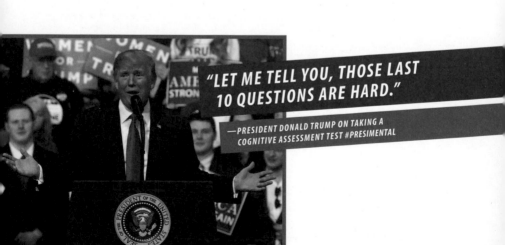

"LET ME TELL YOU, THOSE LAST 10 QUESTIONS ARE HARD."

—PRESIDENT DONALD TRUMP ON TAKING A COGNITIVE ASSESSMENT TEST #PRESIMENTAL

IDENTIFY THE FOLLOWING IMAGES

FILL IN THE OVAL WITH THE CORRECT ANSWER

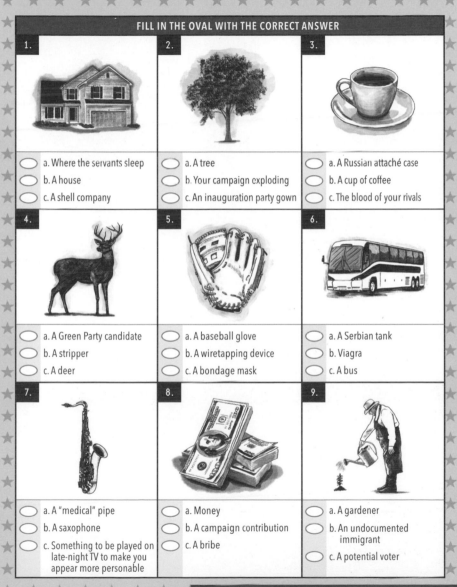

1.
- ○ a. Where the servants sleep
- ○ b. A house
- ○ c. A shell company

2.
- ○ a. A tree
- ○ b. Your campaign exploding
- ○ c. An inauguration party gown

3.
- ○ a. A Russian attaché case
- ○ b. A cup of coffee
- ○ c. The blood of your rivals

4.
- ○ a. A Green Party candidate
- ○ b. A stripper
- ○ c. A deer

5.
- ○ a. A baseball glove
- ○ b. A wiretapping device
- ○ c. A bondage mask

6.
- ○ a. A Serbian tank
- ○ b. Viagra
- ○ c. A bus

7.
- ○ a. A "medical" pipe
- ○ b. A saxophone
- ○ c. Something to be played on late-night TV to make you appear more personable

8.
- ○ a. Money
- ○ b. A campaign contribution
- ○ c. A bribe

9.
- ○ a. A gardener
- ○ b. An undocumented immigrant
- ○ c. A potential voter

ANSWERS: 1. b; 2. a; 3. b; 4. c; 5. a; 6. c; 7. b; 8. a; 9. c

PHYSICAL HEALTH TEST

Not every president has been a picture of physical health. In fact, some are more like that painting of Dorian Gray. But that doesn't mean any slovenly couch potato can hold the office. The daily demands, after all, are great—with little time to sleep or even sit still, stamina is key.

FILL IN THE OVAL THAT BEST APPLIES TO YOU

HOW MUCH EXERCISE DO YOU GET EACH DAY?

- 2 or more hours (100 points)
- 1–2 hours (50 points)
- Less than an hour (25 points)
- Does eating count as exercise? (5 points)

HOW MUCH DIFFICULTY DO YOU HAVE CLIMBING A FLIGHT OF STAIRS?

- None (100 points)
- I get winded (50 points)
- I have to stop multiple times to rest (25 points)
- I quit my job because the office didn't have an elevator (5 points)

DO YOU SMOKE OR CONSUME ALCOHOL?

- Nope (100 points)
- I don't smoke, but I do drink (50 points)
- I smoke, but don't drink (25 points)
- My house is often confused with an Insane Clown Posse concert (5 points)

DO YOU USE MARIJUANA OR OTHER DRUGS?

- Goodness, no (100 points)
- I have in the past in college, but who didn't? (50 points)
- Yes, it's medicinal (25 points)
- Dude, how do we know if purple looks the same to me as it does to you? (5 points)

HOW MUCH CAN YOU LIFT?

- I can move the couch by myself (100 points)
- I can move the ottoman by myself (50 points)
- I can move the laptop by myself (25 points)
- I need help lifting the remote (5 points)

WHICH BEST DESCRIBES YOUR RESTING HEART RATE?

- Like that of a sporting steed (100 points)
- Like that of a sleepy turtle (50 points)
- Like that of a scared bunny (25 points)
- Like that of a cocaine addict in the midst of a HALO jump (5 points)

RESULTS

TOTAL POINTS: _____

550–600: Peak physical condition
400–549: Average health
250–399: Refocus your fitness efforts

31–249: Seek medical attention
0–30: It's possible you are already dead

YOUR PERMANENT RECORD

Just about every presidential candidate has been accused of something terrible. One recent example was the conspiracy theory that Hillary Clinton ran a child sex ring out of a pizza parlor. Though the story was obviously false, some misguided folks actually believed it. More routine accusations include misuse of campaign funds, shady political deals, and sexual assault. And when you get down into the depraved acts allegedly committed by congressional candidates, it's like the freaking Wild West.

Still, no sitting president has ever been convicted of a crime (at least not yet). The closest examples found within the annals of our great nation are Andrew Johnson and Bill Clinton, both of whom were impeached. (More on that later.) And, of course, there's Richard Nixon, whose resignation amid the Watergate scandal so defined presidential malfeasance that "gate" would become the suffix for nearly all ensuing American political scandals (including Hillary Clinton and the aforementioned "Pizzagate").

Eugene V. Debs ran for president from his prison cell at the Atlanta Federal Penitentiary.

There is no explicit language in the Constitution that bars anyone with a criminal record from running for office. In fact, in 1920, a union leader and prominent socialist named Eugene V. Debs ran for president from his prison cell at the Atlanta Federal Penitentiary, where he was serving time for sedition. That said, it's highly inadvisable to use the mugshot from the time you got arrested for drunkenly crashing your Buick 88 into the Piggly Wiggly as your campaign poster.

A clean record is the best record, obviously, so if you're a young person reading this with hopes of running the country one day, stay out of trouble. If you're an adult, turn the page to see some notable criminal offenses that may prove troublesome for your potential campaign.

13

CRIMINAL OFFENSES

FILL IN THE OVALS OF EACH CRIME YOU'VE BEEN CONVICTED OR ACCUSED OF

○ MAYHEM	○ PUBLIC INDECENCY
○ AGGRAVATED MAYHEM	○ DRUG POSSESSION
○ MINOR MAYHEM	○ MONEY LAUNDERING
○ FORCIBLE CONFINEMENT	○ IMPERSONATING AN OFFICER
○ PETTY LARCENY	○ ANIMAL CRUELTY
○ PUBLIC DRUNKENESS	○ BLACKMAIL
○ DRUNK DRIVING	○ POLYGAMY
○ SEX WITH A MINOR	○ TRESPASSING ON FEDERAL LAND
○ MANSLAUGHTER	○ PROSTITUTION
○ MURDER	○ DESTRUCTION OF PUBLIC PROPERTY
○ RECEIVING STOLEN GOODS	○ VANDALISM
○ BREAKING AND ENTERING	○ AGGRAVATED ASSAULT
○ JUST ENTERING	○ REGULAR ASSAULT
○ JUST BREAKING	○ JURY TAMPERING
○ THWARTING BOSS HOGG	○ BEARING FALSE WITNESS
○ GRAND THEFT	○ PUBLIC URINATION
○ GRAND THEFT AUTO	○ PERJURY
○ ARSON	○ TREASON

If you checked two or more boxes, seriously consider shifting your goals to something more realistic, like fry cook or school board member. Even if you checked only one box, you'll likely see that bit of your personal history on the front page of every newspaper and hear it ad nauseam from the lips of your political opponent throughout your campaign. (And you thought your high school yearbook photo was embarrassing.)

NON-CRIMINAL OFFENSES

There are, however, any number of things that are totally legal that could still keep you from winning the presidency. These "non-crimes" are behavioral quirks that won't get you arrested but will likely piss off everyone around you.

FILL IN THE OVALS OF ALL THE NON-CRIMES YOU'VE BEEN CONVICTED OR ACCUSED OF

◯ DRUNK TEXTING	◯ BEING AN AWKWARD HUGGER
◯ SEXTING	◯ TALKING NONSTOP ABOUT CROSSFIT
◯ LITERALLY HAVING SEX WITH YOUR PHONE	◯ SPORTING WORKOUT CLOTHES WITHOUT WORKING OUT
◯ CHEATING ON SPOUSE	◯ CHECKING THE TINDER APP DURING A MEETING
◯ CHEATING AT SCRABBLE	◯ USING AIR QUOTES
◯ DEMONIC POSSESSION	◯ OWNING ANYTHING THAT SAYS "I HATE MONDAYS"
◯ DOUBLE DIPPING	
◯ FAILING TO RECYCLE	◯ PARKING LIKE A JERK
◯ STILL BEING A WOODY ALLEN FAN	◯ SAYING "HASHTAG" BEFORE MAKING A POINT
◯ DRIVING SLOW IN THE FAST LANE	
◯ EATING COWORKER'S LUNCH	◯ FARTING IN AN ELEVATOR
◯ WEARING WHITE AFTER LABOR DAY	◯ PEEING IN THE POOL
◯ LARPing	◯ STARTING A SENTENCE WITH "WELL, ACTUALLY"
◯ BEING AN INTERNET TROLL	◯ STEALING OFFICE SUPPLIES
◯ SPORTING NON-IRONIC MUSTACHE	◯ BUYING BOXED WINE
◯ HATING DOGS	◯ POSTING SPOILERS ON FACEBOOK
◯ ALWAYS SAYING "IT'S RAINING!" WHEN IT RAINS	◯ USING #BLESSED ON EVERY INSTAGRAM POST
◯ HITTING "REPLY ALL" PASSIVE-AGGRESSIVELY	

Any one or combination of the above activities could prove problematic. As stated, they can't keep you from running for office, but they do indicate that you are truly terrible and your staff—the vital lifeblood of any campaign—will eventually turn on you and most likely leak damaging secrets to a pack of wild reporters (or threaten you with blackmail for all eternity).

YOUR IDENTITY

When you run for office, your background will be investigated more thoroughly and subject to more scrutiny than the location of Jimmy Hoffa's body. So, your current gig could serve as a huge advantage…or disadvantage, depending. If you've been elected to a public office, you're way ahead of your slacker competitors. That particular career shows up on the resume of all but one of the first forty-five presidents.

But other vocations could also prove beneficial to your image and ability. Here are a few jobs held by previous U.S. presidents before they took on the big gig. (And before you ding the math, please note that some candidates have been represented more than once since they had multiple work pursuits in the past.)

Without question, everyone who has held the office has had, at some point, a job other than president. So, if you're currently "exploring the employment market," just go get a job. Any job.

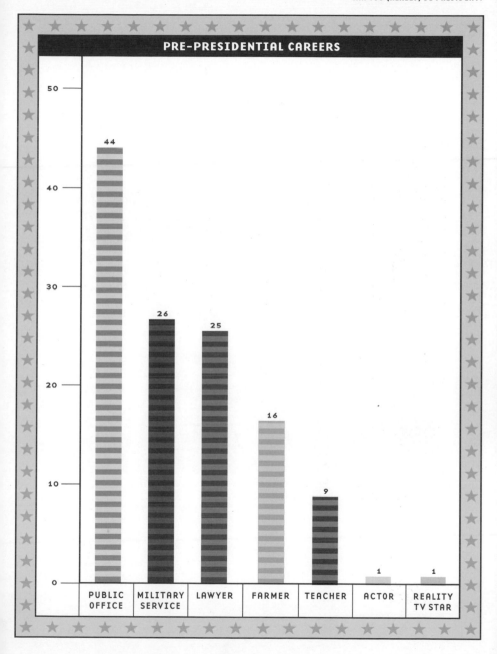

PRE-PRESIDENTIAL CAREERS

Career	Count
PUBLIC OFFICE	44
MILITARY SERVICE	26
LAWYER	25
FARMER	16
TEACHER	9
ACTOR	1
REALITY TV STAR	1

PERSONALITY TYPES

HOW DO YOU IDENTIFY?

Check a box on the following chart to proudly proclaim your identity.

Or don't. It's not important because, no matter how you identify, there's nothing in the U.S. Constitution that says you can't run. Yay!

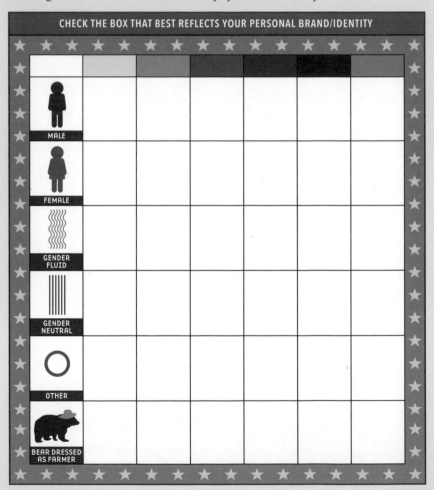

COMMON THREAD

Making decisions that affect national and global policy takes a certain kind of personality. You need a delicate combination of strength, good judgement, trust, skepticism, hope, resolve, intelligence, willingness to learn, and compassion. Unfortunately, pretty much everyone who's either served as or run for president has had only a few of these qualities at best. And some have had little more than a great campaign slogan. (We'll get into that later in the book.)

The one thing all previous presidents and presidential hopefuls do have in common, however, is ego. Lots of ego.

Call it arrogance or vanity or delicately balanced hubris, it is the quality you must have in abundance to get the job. And though there exists a romantic image of the reluctant model citizen who feels called to duty, it's total bullcrap.

It's such a crucial factor that in 2013 a group of psychologists published a study in the journal *Psychological Science* that ranked each of the first forty-two presidents from most narcissistic to least to determine if it could predict professional success or failure. The winner and the nation's leading narcissist was none other than notorious jag-off Lyndon B. Johnson, whose stony pride got us into the Vietnam War. (Last on the list was Millard Fillmore, who only became president because Zachary Taylor died of what scholars believe to be a bad case of the trots.)

Let's elect JIMMY CARTER President

But being president takes more than thinking you have good hair or a fantastic singing voice. You need to truly believe that of all the people in this great nation you are the only one who can correctly lead it. So, do you have the ego to do the job? Let's find out.

> "THERE'S ALWAYS AN ELEMENT OF SELF-DELUSION AMONG PEOPLE WHO BELIEVE THEY OUGHT TO BE PRESIDENT."
>
> —PRESIDENT JIMMY CARTER

CHECK YOUR EGO

FILL IN THE OVAL THAT BEST APPLIES TO YOU

1. YOU'RE IN THE MIDST OF TRYING TO DE-ESCALATE TENSION WITH COMMUNIST COUNTRIES. WHAT DO YOU DO?

- ◯ a. Leave it for another president
- ◯ b. Set up a closed-door diplomatic meeting
- ◯ c. Sleep with Marilyn Monroe

2. YOU'RE TRYING TO BOOST NATIONAL MORALE DURING AN UNPOPULAR WAR. WHAT DO YOU DO?

- ◯ a. Deliver a rousing speech
- ◯ b. Bolster the economy
- ◯ c. Hang a "Mission Accomplished" banner

3. YOU WANT TO QUELL RISING RACIAL TENSIONS. WHAT DO YOU DO?

- ◯ a. Create a social-awareness campaign
- ◯ b. Use stern language in a presidential address
- ◯ c. Hold a "beer summit"

4. YOU FEEL DISCOURAGED BY YOUR UNPOPULARITY AMONG THE POPULACE WHAT DO YOU DO?

- ◯ a. Listen to citizens' concerns and genuinely consider them
- ◯ b. Go on a public relations tour
- ◯ c. Get us into the Vietnam War

5. YOU SEE AN INTERN YOU FIND ATTRACTIVE. WHAT DO YOU DO?

- ◯ a. Silently admire that person, then move on
- ◯ b. Ask for that person's number
- ◯ c. Get a B.J. in the Oval Office

6. YOU'RE GROWING INCREASINGLY CONCERNED ABOUT THE MIGHT OF YOUR POLITICAL RIVALS. WHAT DO YOU DO?

- ◯ a. Challenge them to a debate
- ◯ b. Work with advisors to strengthen your standing
- ◯ c. Have your gang of thugs break into your rivals' offices

7. AN UNFLATTERING STORY ABOUT YOU APPEARS IN A NEWSPAPER. HOW DO YOU RESPOND?

- ◯ a. Have your press secretary issue an educated response
- ◯ b. Ignore it
- ◯ c. Create the blanket term "fake news" and apply it to all such stories

ANSWERS: The correct answer for each is c. If you chose a or b, stop being such a coward.

HOW TO ENLARGE YOUR EGO

If you feel your ego could use some bolstering, this book is here for you. With just a few simple changes in your behavior, you, too, could have the ego of someone like one-time presidential candidate Jonathan Edwards. He famously spent tons of money on haircuts and, even more famously, cheated on his wife, who was dying of cancer, with his personal videographer. C'mon, that's some big ol' brass-balled ego right there. Just ignore the fact that the ensuing scandal essentially nuked his political aspirations and his personal life. Anyway, here are some handy mind-over-matter exercises to help you act egotistical, which will eventually make you feel egotistical and therefore presidential.

★ TALK DOWN TO YOUR SERVER

★ UNFRIEND ANYONE WHO DOESN'T ANSWER THE PHONE WHEN YOU CALL

★ UNFRIEND ANYONE WHO CALLS YOU RATHER THAN TEXTS

★ IGNORE YOUR CHILD BECAUSE YOU HAVE "WORK" TO DO ON YOUR PHONE

★ COMPLAIN LOUDLY WHEN THE LINE AT THE COFFEE SHOP TAKES TOO LONG

★ STOP THE MUSIC AT ANY PARTY YOU ATTEND SO YOU CAN PLAY ACOUSTIC GUITAR FOR EVERYONE

★ TAKE ALL THE PENNIES FROM THE TAKE-A-PENNY DISH AT THE MINI-MART

★ ASSUME EVERYONE YOU MEET WANTS TO SLEEP WITH YOU

★ USE THE PHRASE "I'D LIKE TO TALK TO THE MANAGER" AS OFTEN AS POSSIBLE

★ HONK YOUR HORN ANGRILY AND CONSTANTLY WHEN STUCK IN TRAFFIC

★ CUT PEOPLE OFF AND STEAL PARKING SPOTS

★ REPEATEDLY ASK YOUR VEGAN FRIEND IF THEY CAN EAT CHEESE

★ REFUSE TO HELP WITH HOUSEHOLD CHORES

★ MANSPLAIN THINGS TO WOMEN, EVEN IF YOU ARE A WOMAN

★ WHEN DRIVING, MAKE A RIGHT TURN BEFORE PEOPLE HAVE A CHANCE TO ENTER THE CROSSWALK

★ DON'T PAY IT FORWARD

★ DON'T PAY IT BACK

★ TELL PEOPLE YOU THINK *GAME OF THRONES* IS OVERRATED

★ TELL A TOP CHEF HOW A TRULY GOOD STEAK SHOULD BE PREPARED

★ TALK ABOUT YOUR PROBLEMS AS IF THEY ARE MORE IMPORTANT THAN THOSE OF PEOPLE WITH REAL PROBLEMS

ANGER MANAGEMENT

A healthy ego may boost your chances in a race for the White House, but don't confuse ego with anger. Losing your cool almost never benefits a candidate, even when feeling pissed off is justified.

John Adams famously called George Washington "old mutton-head" while serving as his vice president. Outbursts like that didn't keep him from eventually becoming president, but they did earn him a reputation as a total looney and a crank worthy of numerous scathing biographies and an HBO miniseries. And there's a story of Warren G. Harding nearly choking his own director of the Veterans Bureau in the Oval Office to death. But, really, who hasn't done that? (While not everyone believes that story about Harding, his explosive personality and corrupt presidency have helped solidify it as true in the annals of history.)

But running the country ranks so high on the list of stressful jobs, the only things higher are "bomb defuser" and "Hitler's publicist." So, for your presidential persona, you want to aim for Zen…but not too Zen, lest you come off as some sort of foreigner to the less-traveled, less-experienced voter (also known as a nincompoop). No, you want just the right amount of Zen. Like Matthew McConaughey. You want McConaughey Zen.

To aid you in keeping your anger in check, here are some easy anger management tools for the campaign trail and beyond:

★ DEEP BREATHING

★ MEDITATION

★ HOT YOGA

★ JUST KIND-OF WARM YOGA

★ JOGGING

★ BASKETBALL

★ CALISTHENICS

★ GRECO-ROMAN WRESTLING

★ SCRAPBOOKING

★ BOXING

★ ICE SCULPTING

★ ZUMBA

★ DANCING

★ LISTENING TO MUSIC

★ KNITTING

★ SMOKING POT

YOUR NAME HERE

ECCENTRICS WE CALLED "MR. PRESIDENT"

Like collecting thimbles? Enjoy artisan peanut butter tasting? Spend your afternoons practicing with your zither metal band? Many of our nation's presidents have had notable eccentricities and odd habits. Let's take a look at just a few of these freaks.

SUBVERSIVE SWORDPLAY

George Washington was a pretty fantastic military leader and took great pride in his role as president numero uno—so much so that he felt shaking people's hands was beneath the office. He preferred people bow to him, a gesture that he would then return. It makes sense considering just a short time before he took office we were still bowing to England's King George III. But still, kinda weird. In an effort to keep dignitaries and other officials from simply grabbing his hand, he would keep one hand on his sword and hold his hat with the other. (Passive-aggressive much there, George?)

GOING AL FRESCO

John Quincy Adams (AKA the sixth Beatle) had numerous diplomatic and political accomplishments, including the acquisition of Florida from Spain. So, we have him to thank for America's alligator-infested geographic goiter. In addition to being a real statesman, he also had a reputation as a skinny-dipper. Specifically, he enjoyed swimming in the Potomac River just as the fish did—sans pants.

PANTS FOR DAYS

Speaking of pants, Chester A. Arthur seriously dug them. Like, seriously. As James Garfield's vice president, Arthur took over the big job in 1881 after Garfield was assassinated. He was known as a stalwart politician, even among his rivals. While he worked hard to rid the U.S. Postal Service of corruption and modernize the Navy, he also liked looking dapper. He is rumored to have owned nearly a hundred different pairs of pants and would often change outfits multiple times per day. Hey, just because you're the leader of the free world doesn't mean you can't look FABULOUS!

A CLOSE ENCOUNTER

Former peanut farmer Jimmy Carter spent most of his presidency dealing with a hostage crisis and the aftermath of an oil embargo and shortage. But before any of that, he claimed to have seen a UFO. Around the time he served as governor of Georgia, he observed a strange light in the sky one night that quickly disappeared. Though he never said he thought it was an actual alien craft, he still filed an official report about the event.

Yes, each of these weirdos managed to serve the nation despite their funny little quirks. And considering we're talking about a social neophyte, a nudist, a clotheshorse, and a total nutter (pun intended), you should feel free to run for president no matter the odd skeletons in your closet (as long as they're not actual skeletons).

LET'S REVIEW

PRACTICE TEST

Let's review what you've learned so far about presidential personalities and behavior with this semi-handy fill-in-the-blanks quiz. If you want a real challenge, have a friend or spouse or campaign manager hold the quiz and ask you to supply the requested fill-in words with absolutely no context other than the listed category (i.e., noun, verb, etc.). Y'know, like that fun game you played as a kid that we can't mention by name for legal reasons.

FILL IN THE BLANKS

When it comes to being _____ (GOVERNMENT JOB TITLE), everyone has their own _____ (NOUN). For example, George Washington made visitors _____ (VERB) to him because he believed shaking _____ (PLURAL NOUN) was beneath the _____ (NOUN). But that seems a harmless _____ (NOUN) considering Warren G. Harding was caught _____ (PRESENT PARTICIPLE VERB) his own _____ (GOVERNMENT JOB TITLE) in the _____ (NAME OF A PLACE). Of course, neither had the _____ (NOUN) of Lyndon B. Johnson, who is considered the most _____ (ADJECTIVE) of all of the presidents. One thing can be _____ (PAST TENSE VERB) about all of them, however, and that is each had a chance to _____ (VERB) this great country and leave their _____ (NOUN) in the _____ (SCHOOL SUBJECT) books. Let's just hope we don't end up like Zachary Taylor, though, who died of _____ (INTESTINAL PROBLEM).

PRESIDENTIAL ELIGIBILITY TEST

Now that we've gone over the basics, let's check your potential eligibility. The following test will…uh…test your knowledge of what we've covered so far and how it applies to your potential campaign. Once you complete it, you'll have a handy-dandy sheet, suitable for laminating, that displays your strengths (and weaknesses).

	FILL IN ALL OVALS THAT APPLY
1. OFFICIAL REQUIREMENTS	
◯	a. I am a natural-born citizen of the United States of America
◯	b. I am at least 35-years-old
◯	c. I have lived in the United States of America for 14 consecutive years
2. MENTAL HEALTH	
◯	a. I have good mental health
◯	b. I can identify basic shapes and items, but struggle with larger concepts
◯	c. I'm crazier than a craphouse rat
3. PHYSICAL HEALTH	
◯	a. I am physically healthy
◯	b. I am of average physical health
◯	c. I ate a block of Wisconsin extra-sharp cheddar for breakfast
4. EXPERIENCE	
◯	a. I've held public office and/or served in the military
◯	b. I've held public office and/or served as a lawyer
◯	c. What is "employment" anyway?

5. YOUR CRIMINAL RECORD

- ◯ a. I have no criminal record
- ◯ b. I have no criminal record yet
- ◯ c. I'm a straight-up gangsta

6. YOUR NON-CRIMINAL RECORD

- ◯ a. I have no annoying qualities
- ◯ b. I have some annoying qualities
- ◯ c. I'm the person everyone in the office hates

7. EGO-LEVEL

- ◯ a. I have a civic duty to lead my country
- ◯ b. I feel I am owed the job of president
- ◯ c. This'll show Vanessa she should've gone with me to the prom

8. TEMPERAMENT

- ◯ a. I am usually calm and collected
- ◯ b. I have occasional outbursts
- ◯ c. SCREW YOU! IT'S NONE OF YOUR DAMN BUSINESS!

Vote for [your name here].

27

CHAPTER 2

BUILDING YOUR CAMPAIGN

[YOUR
FACE
HERE]

PICK YOUR TEAM

REPUBLICANS, DEMOCRATS, AND "OTHER"

Before you step out onto the campaign trail, you're going to need to know your party affiliation. What? You thought you needed to know what you stand for first? Nope. That's a common misconception. If history has taught us anything, it's that you pick a lane then determine for what you stand. And even then, you only do that after countless focus groups, donor meetings, polls, more donor meetings, backroom deals, even more donor meetings, and so on. So, let's get that cart back behind the donkey.

It can be stupidly difficult to figure out whether you're a Republican, a Democrat, or something else altogether because, quite frankly, the tent-pole causes for which each party fights are constantly in flux and subject to a variety of factors that include everything from which party controls the House or Senate (more on what those are later) to what some random political commentator had for breakfast.

And it gets even more confusing when you consider a hundred years ago each party basically stood for the opposite of what they do now. Scholars think this flip happened sometime around the turn of the twentieth century as both parties adopted different platforms to woo new voters. Crazy, huh? So, we'll use today's political temperature as a guide with the knowledge that this may all change.

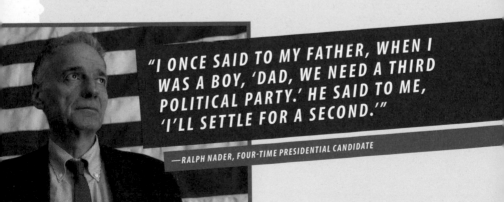

"I ONCE SAID TO MY FATHER, WHEN I WAS A BOY, 'DAD, WE NEED A THIRD POLITICAL PARTY.' HE SAID TO ME, 'I'LL SETTLE FOR A SECOND.'"

—RALPH NADER, FOUR-TIME PRESIDENTIAL CANDIDATE

POP QUIZ!
WHICH POLITICAL AFFILIATION IS RIGHT FOR YOU?

FILL IN THE OVAL THAT BEST APPLIES TO YOU

YOUR FAVORITE SNACK IS
- a. Grilled chicken with capers and lemongrass
- b. Steak with ketchup
- c. Grilled venison I killed myself
- d. Tofurkey and brown rice
- e. All-you-can-eat chili bar

YOUR FAVORITE BOOK IS
- a. *To Kill a Mockingbird*
- b. *The Bible*
- c. *Lord of the Flies*
- d. *An Inconvenient Truth*
- e. *The Metamorphosis*

YOUR FAVORITE MOVIE IS
- a. *Citizen Kane*
- b. *Mr. Smith Goes to Washington*
- c. *Red Dawn*
- d. Anything directed by Robert Altman
- e. *Fritz the Cat*

YOUR FAVORITE COLOR IS
- a. Blue
- b. Red
- c. Purple
- d. Green
- e. Rainbow sparkles

YOU ARE INTERESTED IN
- a. Civil rights
- b. Gun rights
- c. Personal freedom
- d. Pot
- e. The truth about Area 51

IF YOU HAD $50 MILLION, YOU'D
- a. Donate it to the ACLU
- b. Build one of those Christian hospitals
- c. Finish my survivalist compound
- d. Buy an antiwhaling vessel
- e. Put it in my mattress

WHEN THINGS GET TOUGH, YOU
- a. Reach across the aisle
- b. Look to history for guidance
- c. Stockpile provisions
- d. Chain yourself to a tree
- e. Pray to Zeus

YOUR BIGGEST STRENGTH IS YOUR
- a. Sense of civic duty
- b. Sense of justice
- c. Sense of independence
- d. Sense of global responsibility
- e. Sense of superiority

YOU WISH YOU WERE BETTER AT
- a. Public relations
- b. Connecting with blue-collar workers
- c. Explaining my platform
- d. Fundraising
- e. Making protest signs

YOUR FAVORITE SONG IS
- a. "This Is America" by Childish Gambino
- b. "The Dance" by Garth Brooks
- c. "The Star-Spangled Banner" by Francis S. Key
- d. Whatever song the drum circle is playing
- e. Music is evil

RESULTS

If you picked 7 or more in a given category, your affiliation is:
a = Democrat   b = Republican   c = Libertarian   d = Green Party

If you picked some other combination/total, you're some sort of freak who's gonna need some more guidance. (See next page.)

ON THE "OTHER" HAND

Candidates who fall into the "Other" bucket tend to struggle to keep up with the juggernaut campaigns of Repubs and Dems. The good news is, when it comes to "Other," you have a whole host of parties to choose from, including (but not limited to):

- ★ TEA PARTY
- ★ PIRATE*
- ★ NEW BLACK PANTHER
- ★ LEGAL MARIJUANA NOW**
- ★ SOCIALIST

- ★ PROGRESSIVE
- ★ MODERN WHIG
- ★ COMMUNIST
- ★ KEY***

*Totally true.   **Also true.   ***Not a political party, but they're fun.

"OTHER" LIKES AND DISLIKES

The Tea Party, Progressive, and Socialist parties have gained a lot of traction recently, which is incredible considering "socialist" was considered a synonym for "enemy of the state" for much of the late-twentieth century. Here's a quick cheat sheet:

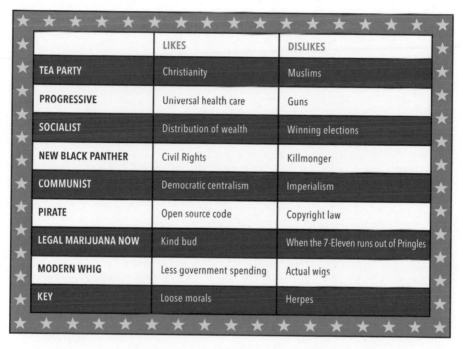

	LIKES	DISLIKES
TEA PARTY	Christianity	Muslims
PROGRESSIVE	Universal health care	Guns
SOCIALIST	Distribution of wealth	Winning elections
NEW BLACK PANTHER	Civil Rights	Killmonger
COMMUNIST	Democratic centralism	Imperialism
PIRATE	Open source code	Copyright law
LEGAL MARIJUANA NOW	Kind bud	When the 7-Eleven runs out of Pringles
MODERN WHIG	Less government spending	Actual wigs
KEY	Loose morals	Herpes

And this list doesn't even feature the horrible parties that everyone thought were obliterated by a roguish archeology professor in the 1940s (cough-cough-NAZIS!-cough).

Of course, you could always go with Independent, which allows you to pick and choose elements from various political platforms while not being beholden to any of them. And if you think independent candidates have no checks in the win column, George Washington was technically an independent, having no affiliation with any political party of the time. Other moderately successful independent presidential candidates include Ross Perot, Ralph Nader, and Bernie Sanders. (It also sounds cool, much like "independent music" and "independent film" and "independently wealthy" do.)

PICK YOUR PLATFORM

OK, so about that pesky platform—the cause that will come to define you and your campaign—let's keep it simple, shall we? Because we all know no one really cares deeply about the issues. Superficially maybe, but deeply? LOL, nope.

Just focus on being at least moderately likable* and select from the following collection of noble causes by closing your eyes and pointing at the page.

SMALLER GOVERNMENT   CYBER TERRORISM
THE IRISH   ENVIRONMENTALISM   LGBT RIGHTS   CLONING   NORTH KOREA
GMO FOOD   SECURING BORDERS   NATIONAL SECURITY   IMPORTS   EXPORTS
HOMELESS   MANUFACTURING   2ND AMENDMENT   EDUCATION
EQUAL PAY
PRO-LIFE   EXPLORING SPACE   VETERANS
PRO-CHOICE   IMMIGRATION   ISIS   IRAN
GLOBAL TRADE   TACKLE RACISM
TERRORISM   NUCLEAR THREATS
TAX BREAKS
CLEAN COAL   TAX REFORM   MIDDLE CLASS
CHIPMUNKS
ALTERNATIVE ENERGY   NATIONAL DEBT   CRIME
RECYCLING   GRAFFITI   FREE COLLEGE
BANKING SYSTEM   INFRASTRUCTURE   MINIMUM WAGE
RELIGIOUS FREEDOM   STATES RIGHTS   MONOPOLIES
PRISON REFORM   TECHNICAL INNOVATION   SAVE WHALES
FUNDING MILITARY   CONTACTING ALIENS   1ST AMENDMENT

*You can be an dirtbag, just not a total dirtbag.

CAMPAIGN BASICS

WOOING YOUR BASE

Now that you've picked your party and your platform, it's time to energize your base. And sadly, your base is not a secret lair where you torture British secret agents before tossing them into a vat filled with angry piranhas. No, your base is your core group of voters—the ones who'll help get out your message, fill your rallies, get into heated arguments with supporters of your competition while in line at Starbucks, and (most importantly) vote for you.

The keys to motivating and mobilizing your base are simple:

KEEP IT PERSONAL   Tell stories about people they'll never meet to make your point seem more real. Don't talk about George Clooney, though, but rather "Kathy Harrison, a mom with three kids." No one knows who Kathy Harrison is, but they'll relate to her story of struggling to pay medical bills or whatever.

KEEP IT VAGUE   Use lofty terms and metaphors to make your base feel excited, but don't tell them what you actually plan to do, y'know, like when then-candidate George H. W. Bush said, "Read my lips. No. New. Taxes." Campaign promises always fall short in the end because getting things done as president is pretty much a crap shoot as ol' Bush Sr. learned when, as president, he had to enact new taxes.

KEEP IT FAMILIAR   Tell them what they already know—or what they think they know. Don't challenge them to try to see anything from another perspective. Though voters say they do, most don't like to consider anyone else's point of view. It sounds cynical, but this is science, people.

YOUR CAMPAIGN STAFF

A presidential campaign has a lot of moving parts. Seriously, like, think of a watch with all of its intricate gears and cogs. Now think of a big watch made up of hundreds of smaller watches…This isn't the greatest metaphor, but you get what I'm saying. There's a lot going on, and it ever stops.

Your campaign staff keeps you on track, on time, and on point. We'll just discuss the top-level folks but understand that each of the following positions manages a team of people, who in turn manage their own teams, and so on, and so on, all the way down to the local volunteers who knock on doors in their hometown. So, y'know, it's all connected. Like *The Matrix*.

"POLITICS IS A MESSY BUSINESS, BUT CAMPAIGNING PREPARES YOU FOR GOVERNING. IT PREPARES YOU TO GET HIT, STAND STRONG AND, IF NECESSARY, HIT BACK."

—JAMES CARVILLE, CAMPAIGN MANAGER FOR BILL CLINTON

★ CAMPAIGN DIRECTOR

Basically, the person running the show, who oversees all aspects of the campaign and campaign staff. Just do whatever they say.

★ POLITICAL DIRECTOR

Finds local and national organizations that align with your platform to help expand your base and forge alliances, like a dating app for dollar bills.

★ FINANCE CHAIRPERSON

This is the big money person who works with large donors to secure funding for the campaign (not to be confused with the Fundraising Director, who is the small money person). This person puts the "ick" in politics.

★ FIELD DIRECTOR

Manages the volunteer staff and voter awareness and registration initiatives. Think of this person as the gang leader, minus the gang sign.

★ FUNDRAISING DIRECTOR

Organizes donation drives and events and keeps the campaign from breaking any fundraising laws—and that keeps you out of jail.

★ COMMUNICATIONS DIRECTOR

Crafts the media narrative for the campaign, can oversee or also function as Press Secretary. This person is supposed to keep you from looking or sounding too stupid.

★ CAMPAIGN TREASURER

Keeps track of all of the money coming in and going out, unless you're bribing someone. They probably wouldn't track that.

CAMPAIGN ETIQUETTE

OK, your staff is in place. Now don't screw this up. The door to your campaign headquarters should not be a revolving one. High turnover can spell disaster for a presidential campaign (or a sitting president), so you need to keep your staff inspired, passionate, and engaged. How do you do that? Here are some basics that'll help you keep the folks on your team a part of your team.

★ **DO ENGAGE IN LIGHT CONVERSATION WITH THEM**

★ **DO NOT ENGAGE IN HEAVY PETTING WITH THEM**

★ **DO OFFER WORDS OF ENCOURAGEMENT AND PRAISE**

★ **DO NOT OFFER "YOUR MAMA" JOKES**

★ **DO LISTEN TO IDEAS FROM YOUR STAFFERS**

★ **DO NOT LISTEN TO CRIMINAL CONFESSIONS FROM YOUR STAFFERS**

★ **DO BRING IN SPECIAL TREATS, LIKE DONUTS OR COFFEE**

★ **DO NOT BRING IN BLOW**

★ **DO ACKNOWLEDGE THEY WORK LONG HOURS**

★ **DO NOT ACKNOWLEDGE MOST OF THEM WON'T BE PAID**

★ **DO LEAD BY EXAMPLE**

★ **DO NOT LEAD BY SCREAMING**

★ **DO REMAIN PROFESSIONAL AND COURTEOUS**

★ **DO NOT FORGET YOUR PANTS**

WHEN THINGS GO WRONG

Of course, it's unrealistic to assume everything will be strawberry skies and magical unicorn farts the whole time. There will certainly come a time (or multiple times) when you need to bring the proverbial hammer down to demonstrate your passion. Though we've covered the importance and benefits of anger management, in instances like this, the most effective action to take is flipping a table. Tables are sturdy and won't break, and they make a huge noise when upended.

To effectively flip a table for impact:

- ★ PLACE STACKS OF PAPERS AND OTHER LIGHT ITEMS ON TOP (WHEN STUFF GOES AIRBORNE, IT PROVIDES A RICHER TABLE-FLIPPING EXPERIENCE FOR ALL)

- ★ ENSURE ANY CHAIRS AROUND THE TABLE ARE WHEELED OFFICE CHAIRS SO THAT WITNESSES CAN EASILY AND QUICKLY ROLL AWAY

- ★ DO SOME STRETCHES BEFORE PEOPLE ENTER THE ROOM

- ★ POSITION YOURSELF ON A WIDE SIDE OF THE TABLE (FLIPPING THE TABLE LENGTHWISE IS AN ADVANCED MOVE)

- ★ CALL IN AS MANY STAFF MEMBERS AS WILL SAFELY FIT IN THE ROOM (BE SURE TO ALLOW ENOUGH PACE FOR SEATED FOLKS TO ROLL OUT OF THE WAY)

- ★ AS YOU SPEAK, RAMP UP THE EMOTION. POUND ON THE TABLE FOR EFFECT

- ★ WHEN READY, GRAB THE UNDERSIDE OF THE TABLETOP, PALMS UP

- ★ LIFT WITH YOUR KNEES, NOT YOUR BACK

- ★ YELL

- ★ RAISE THE TABLE THROUGH A ROTATIONAL AXIS UNTIL YOU FEEL GRAVITY TAKE OVER

- ★ STORM OUT

In addition to snapping your staffers back into shape, this act will also grant you about thirty minutes of solo time because no one will want to go near you. The downside is they will think you are completely off your nut.

WHEN THINGS GO RIGHT

You will spend a great deal of time with your campaign staff, often late at night in various hotel or motel rooms. Given the intense schedule and emotion that comes with a presidential campaign, it's perfectly natural for romantic feelings to arise between yourself and one (or perhaps many) of your staff or interns or volunteers. Should these urges begin to stir in you, you must consider the potential outcome. I mean, it goes without saying that nothing you do should enrage anyone to the point of creating a hashtag and/or social justice movement. But could it be real love? Here are the steps to determine how to embark upon a campaign romance:

STEP 1

★ **DON'T**

STEP 2

★ **JUST DON'T**

CAMPAIGN MESSAGING

Though your campaign platform may include a complex set of ideas and solutions, you'll want to boil all of that down into a simple phrase or hashtag that people can easily remember and that will fit on a button or embroidered hat. After all, when at a rally, it's difficult for attendees to enthusiastically shout "Our oil imports in the global trade market represent a dangerous percentage when compared to our gross domestic product, especially considering our economic reliance on the exports of electronics and similar goods, and therefore we should offset this with a focus on renewable energy innovation to help stabilize the future of our national economy!"

See? It doesn't quite roll off of the tongue. Thankfully, the campaign slogan tackles that problem. In the past, these catchphrases have ranged from alliterative (William McKinley's 1896 slogan: "Patriotism, Protection, and Prosperity") to insulting (Henry Clay's 1844 slogan: "Who is James K. Polk?") to downright goofy (Dwight Eisenhower's 1952 slogan: "I like Ike").

There's nothing in Reagan's 1984 "It's Morning Again in America" campaign materials that mentioned the sunrise or pancakes or drinking coffee while sitting on the toilet, all of which are morning things.

Recent history, however, has favored vague platitudes—combinations of words that sound meaningful when strung together but are empty enough for people to fill with their own patriotic definition, like Ronald Reagan's 1984 slogan "It's Morning Again in America." Seriously, what the #@$! does that even mean? His campaign focused largely on bolstering the U.S. economy. There's nothing in his campaign materials that mentioned the sunrise or pancakes or drinking coffee while sitting on the toilet, all of which are morning things.

Rather than have your staff grind away on the right combination of uplifting but non-specific words, simply use this campaign slogan generator on the next page and start printing T-shirts. Let's go sloganing!

CAMPAIGN SLOGAN GENERATOR

CHOOSE FROM EACH SECTION TO CREATE YOUR CAMPAIGN SLOGAN BELOW

CHOOSE THE FIRST LETTER OF YOUR FIRST NAME		ADD THE FIRST LETTER OF YOUR LAST NAME		THEN PICK YOUR FAVORITE COLOR	
A	GRANT	A	THE COUNTRY	RED	THE FUTURE
B	BUILD	B	EACH OF US	GRAY	A NEW DAY
C	OFFER	C	YOUR NEIGHBOR	MAUVE	HOPE
D	PROMISE	D	THE LAND OF THE FREE	PINK	PRIDE
E	SEE	E	THE PEOPLE	BRONZE	FREEDOM
F	SHOW	F	BABIES	GREEN	EXPERIENCE
G	DENY	G	THE NATION	PURPLE	GREATNESS
H	HAND	H	THE MOTHERLAND	FUCHSIA	STRENGTH
I	ADMIT	I	EVERYONE	BLACK	HEALTH
J	ALLOW	J	THE CITIZENS	YELLOW	BREAKFAST
K	WIN	K	OUR VETERANS	TEAL	AUTHORITY
L	GIVE	L	THIS LAND	OLIVE	AN EDUCATION
M	DECLARE	M	YOUR RIGHTS	BROWN	A PATH FORWARD
N	RESPECT	N	SOCIETY	LAVENDER	PEACE
O	PROFESS	O	OUR NATION	FOREST	ALLEGIANCE
P	WIN	P	THE UNION	WHITE	A NEW TOMORROW
Q	DELIVER	Q	OUR CHILDREN	BEIGE	CONFIDENCE
R	EARN	R	THE CONSTITUTION	MAROON	A BRIGHTER DAY
S	SUPPLY	S	AMERICA	SEA GREEN	PROSPERITY
T	INDULGE	T	EVERY GENERATION	ORANGE	DURING WARTIME
U	PRESENT	U	OUR COUNTRY	GOLD	WEALTH
V	BESTOW	V	DEMOCRACY	EGG SHELL	GUNS
W	PROVIDE	W	THE UNITED STATES	AQUA BLUE	LOVE
X	BEQUEATH	X	THE YOUTH	SILVER	FAITH
Y	BRING	Y	YOUR HOME	PEACH	POWER
Z	AWARD	Z	THE MAJORITY	BLUE	FIERCENESS

RESULTS

YOUR CAMPAIGN SLOGAN IS: _____

NOW, HASHTAG IT: #_____

43

WHO'S GOING TO PAY FOR ALL THIS?

Campaigns ain't cheap. You'll need to cover travel, salaries, office supplies, office space, food, consultants, posters, cell phones, and a ton of other things. Needless to say, you can't just get a summer job at Baskin-Robbins to pay for it all. No, you'll need a lot of money. Like, a stupid amount of money.

It should be noted that option three below only worked for Calvin Coolidge, our thirtieth president and alleged witch sympathizer*. For that reason, we'll stick to options one and two.

If you plan on going the fundraising route, your finance chairperson and fundraising director play a major role in whether or not you're flying first class or riding a Greyhound to your next campaign stop. And while you may think the key to success lies in scoring large donors, keep in mind that fundraising drives like those of Howard Dean and Bernie Sanders raised millions thanks to individual donations of one-hundred dollars or less.

THE 3 BEST WAYS TO HANDLE CAMPAIGN COSTS

1. FUNDRAISING

2. PAY FOR IT YOURSELF

3. GET A WITCH TO CAST A MONEY SPELL

*Alleged by some guy shouting through a bullhorn from his van plastered with Bible verses, parked in front of a liquor store.

HOW TO RAISE CAMPAIGN FUNDS

There are so many rules and laws that govern how you can raise money, how you can spend it, and where you can put it, you'll need to tread carefully—or just know the way around most of that, which we'll cover in a bit. First, let's examine the basic steps to successfully raising campaign funds:

SELF-FINANCING

Most political veterans caution against using your own money to finance your campaign. This makes sense because, if you don't make it all the way to the White House, it's better to lose someone else's money than your own. That said, if you have money and want to just go for it, you can contribute as much as you want to yourself. For this to work, you must:

★ BE RICH

If you're not already rich, however, here are a few ways you can quickly amass a huge fortune:

★ INVEST IN A COMPANY THAT'S ABOUT TO BE BONKERS SUCCESSFUL

★ GET ADOPTED BY A RICH PERSON

★ WIN THE LOTTERY

Please try to avoid these get-rich-quick schemes as they often don't work and most of them are illegal:

★ SELL YOUR ORGANS

★ SELL SOMEONE ELSE'S ORGANS

★ GET INTO THE DRUG TRADE

★ USE ALCHEMY TO TURN LEAD INTO GOLD

★ START A BLOG

★ CONVINCE BILL GATES TO INVEST IN A PONZI SCHEME

THE PAC: SUPER AND OTHERWISE

There is a third option. You may have heard of something called a Political Action Committee (PAC) or its cousin from Krypton, the Super PAC. These organizations have become key factors in whether a candidate wins or loses an election. And like most election-related processes, they're shady as shiz.

A regular PAC basically tries to help or defeat a certain candidate without actually being affiliated with said candidate. There are limits on how much people and groups can donate to a given PAC ($5,000 annual limit per entity or individual) and how much that PAC can donate to a campaign ($5,000 per election and/or $15,000 to a national party per year). There are lots of other limits and rules and laws and, quite frankly, I could list them all and we'd be here all day getting into the minutiae. Or we could do what pretty much all politicians have done and move onto Super PACs.

There are almost no rules for Super PACs. Though they can't make direct donations to campaigns or committees, they have no donation limit (either coming in or going out). So, they usually use the seemingly unlimited funding to craft hit pieces on opposing candidates that wade so far into the mud the staff needs scuba gear.

And there are laws that keep candidates from coordinating with PACs and Super PACs but, y'know, it's like the samples at Costco. You're only supposed to take one, but everyone just stands there stuffing their gobs anyway. I'm not saying you should break the law during your campaign, I'm just saying not everyone in a campaign fights fair. So be warned.

Oh, and Super PACs are idiotically simple to set up. With a bank account and a simple five-sheet document, you can create your own Super PAC and add it to this partial list of ridiculous yet actual Super Pac names[3]:

★ THIS IS WHY WE CAN'T HAVE NICE THINGS

★ EMPIRE STRIKES PAC

★ SCIENCE!

★ BEARS FOR A BEARABLE TOMORROW, TODAY

★ AMERICANS FOR A BETTER TODAY, TODAY

★ AMERICANS AGAINST DIET MOUNTAIN DEW

★ BABY GOT PAC

★ CAN YOU NOT

★ CITIZENS FOR A RESILIENT AMERICA AND PIZZA

★ DEVILS FOR GOOD

★ DON'T APPROVE THIS SUPER PAC

★ SERIOUSLY, DON'T APPROVE THIS SUPER PAC

★ YOUNG SWINDLERS OF TOMORROW

★ I'M BRINGING SEXY PAC

★ JUST DRINK THE KOOL-AID

★ MAKE AMERICA DANK AGAIN

★ THE RAT PAC

★ WE CAN DO IT, YOU GUYS! PROBABLY.

★ WHY NOT ZOID PAC?

Write the name of your potential Super PAC…uh, I mean the name of a potential Super PAC, not yours because that would be illegal, here:

_____

[3]Center for Responsive Politics. 2018 Outside Spending, by Super PAC

DEBATE PREPARATION

Performance at a debate can win or lose the election. Sure, I've said that before. But we're talking about debates. Stay focused! There are two components to a debate:

1. KNOWLEDGE OF THE ISSUES

2. WHAT TO DO WITH YOUR HANDS

While the former should take precedent over the latter, the latter has increasingly proven important considering some debate formats allow for people to not just use their hands but gallivant all over the stage. But we'll focus on the hands later in the Appearing Presidential section of the book. For now, let's talk talking.

First, you must have a deep knowledge of the issues. Whatever topics come up, you should demonstrate the ability to speak about them as if you are an expert. "As if" is the key here. There's no way you could be a real expert on everything, you just need to know enough to fake it. Not only should you have "concrete" facts and stats (that's in quotes because you can find any facts and stats to back up your argument, even if that argument is "why we should eat children"), but you'll need to deftly and smoothly transition conversation

about one topic to another of your preference (aka "pivot"). Here's an example:

Moderator: "What would you do to lower the national crime rate?"

Candidate: "Well, as you know there were an estimated 1.2 million violent crimes in our country last year. So, I'd work closely with local law enforcement officials the same way I've worked with state and federal Veterans Affairs offices to provide our military heroes the tools and funding they need to help clear the backlog of medical claims."

Boom. Command of the facts and a total redirect. Doing this takes a lot of practice—I mean, a transition like that done incorrectly could lead you to pull a hammy or something. Thankfully, your staff will run you through a bunch of mock debates and hire a consultant of some kind to get you in fighting shape. You should also put the *Rocky III* soundtrack on a loop in your campaign office.

THE FOURTH ESTATE AND YOU

Many political candidates have a relationship with the press that would make a great rom-com. They hate the press, they love the press, the press thinks the politicians are too private, the politicians think the press is too clingy—just kiss already!

Whatever your thoughts on the role of reporters in the political process, consider this observation from journalist and author Amy Goodman. She said, "Journalism is the only profession explicitly protected by the U.S. Constitution because journalists are supposed to be the check and balance on government." The quote goes on to slam corporate media, but let that first part sink in. If you're running for president, you have to deal with the media and not always on your terms. So, let's make the best of it, shall we?

In a campaign, everything will get reported. And I mean everything—your daily schedule, your boring press releases, what you had for lunch and where you had it, the football team you're rooting for, how you take your coffee, if you say "bless you" or "gesundheit" when someone sneezes. Ev. Ery. Thing. That said, most of that kind of stuff will be dumped into pretty mundane pieces that get buried on A9 next to the ad for the weekend sale at the Mattress Emporium. It may sound boring and reporters agree.

"WERE IT LEFT TO ME TO DECIDE WHETHER WE SHOULD HAVE A GOVERNMENT WITHOUT NEWSPAPERS OR NEWSPAPERS WITHOUT A GOVERNMENT, I SHOULD NOT HESITATE FOR A MOMENT TO PREFER THE LATTER."

—PRESIDENT THOMAS JEFFERSON

That's why they're constantly looking for something more interesting. Accidentally say something racist? They'll jump on it. Insult the local high school mascot? It'll go on the front page. Have an affair with a campaign aide? It's like manna from heaven. Heck, during a debate Rick Perry forgot the name of one of the three federal agencies he planned to eliminate when president (it was the Department of Energy) and his campaign never recovered from the media blowback.

All of that said, you need the media. They help spread your message and can even play a hand in the success of your campaign. So, work with your Communications Director on the narrative(s) you want to portray and how to make that happen. When crafting that narrative, I advise you to stay away from mentions of dragon and wizards or any other sci-fi/fantasy elements. It'll make you sound like you're fresh out of the nuthouse, even though people love that crap.

CAMPAIGN TRAIL CROSSWORD

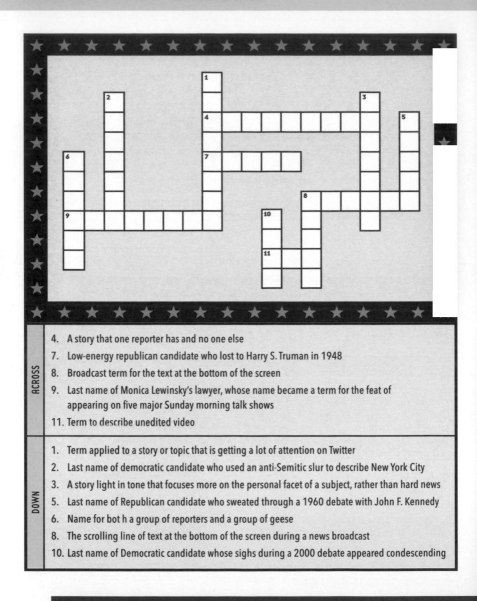

ACROSS

4. A story that one reporter has and no one else
7. Low-energy republican candidate who lost to Harry S. Truman in 1948
8. Broadcast term for the text at the bottom of the screen
9. Last name of Monica Lewinsky's lawyer, whose name became a term for the feat of appearing on five major Sunday morning talk shows
11. Term to describe unedited video

DOWN

1. Term applied to a story or topic that is getting a lot of attention on Twitter
2. Last name of democratic candidate who used an anti-Semitic slur to describe New York City
3. A story light in tone that focuses more on the personal facet of a subject, rather than hard news
5. Last name of Republican candidate who sweated through a 1960 debate with John F. Kennedy
6. Name for bot h a group of reporters and a group of geese
8. The scrolling line of text at the bottom of the screen during a news broadcast
10. Last name of Democratic candidate whose sighs during a 2000 debate appeared condescending

ANSWERS: 1. Trending; 2. Jackson; 3. Feature; 4. Exclusive; 5. Nixon;6. Gaggle; 7. Dewey; 8. (Across) Chyron; 8. (Down) Crawl; 9. Ginsberg; 10. Gore; 11. Raw

LET'S REVIEW

PRACTICE TEST

OK, time to see whether or not you're campaign-trail ready. Even if you fail miserably, don't worry. Most of the past presidential candidates would probably fail this test too. And some of them went on to win the election.

DRAW A LINE TO CONNECT THE JOB TITLE TO THE APPROPRIATE DESCRIPTION

Job Title	Description
FINANCE CHAIRPERSON	Person with whom you should definitely not have an affair
FEATURES REPORTER	Manages campaign volunteers and voter registration initiatives
CAMPAIGN INTERN	Finds local and national organizations that align with your platform
INDIE MUSICIAN	Works with large donors to secure funding for your campaign
FIELD DIRECTOR	Creates light personal stories for a news outlet
POLITICAL DIRECTOR	Someone who can ask their own fan base to donate to your campaign

ANSWERS: FINANCE CHAIRPERSON: Works with large donors; FEATURES REPORTER: Creates light personal stories; CAMPAIGN INTERN: Person with whom; INDIE MUSICIAN: Someone who can ask; FIELD DIRECTOR: Manages campaign volunteers; POLITICAL DIRECTOR: Finds local and national organizations

PRESIDENTIAL CAMPAIGN TEST

All right. Now that you've learned the nuts and bolts of a successful campaign, let's test your mastery of it all. Usually, this is when most would say something reassuring like "and there are no wrong answers," but there totally are wrong answers.

FILL IN ALL OVALS THAT APPLY

1. YOUR POLITICAL AFFILIATION IS

- ◯ a. Republican
- ◯ b. Democrat
- ◯ c. Libertarian
- ◯ d. Green
- ◯ e. Whatever gets me elected

2. ONE OF THE COMPONENTS OF A GOOD SPEECH IS

- ◯ a. Mentioning George Clooney
- ◯ b. Terms and metaphors that excite, but don't explain what you actually plan to do
- ◯ c. Pantomime

3. THE STAFF MEMBER WHO TRACKS DONATIONS COMING IN AND MONEY GOING OUT

- ◯ a. The Political Director
- ◯ b. The Campaign Treasurer
- ◯ c. The Communications Director
- ◯ d. A Russian oligarch

4. AN EXAMPLE OF BAD CAMPAIGN ETIQUETTE IS MOST LIKELY

- ◯ a. Listening to ideas from your staffers
- ◯ b. Remaining professional and courteous
- ◯ c. Telling hackers to attack your opponent

5. REGARDING A ROMANTIC OR SEXUAL LIAISON WITH A STAFFER, YOU SHOULD

- ◯ a. Prepare for negative reactions
- ◯ b. Avoid it at all costs
- ◯ c. Wear something sexy

6. RECENT CAMPAIGN SLOGANS HAVE FAVORED

- a. Vague platitudes
- b. Specifics
- c. Ocelots

7. THE LEAST RECOMMENDED METHOD OF CAMPAIGN FUNDRAISING IS

- a. Fundraising
- b. Paying for it yourself
- c. Printing your own money

8. SUPER PACS HAVE

- a. No spending or donation limit
- b. Less spending freedom than a regular PAC
- c. An all-you-can-eat chicken-wing bar

9. FOR A SUCCESSFUL DEBATE PERFORMANCE, YOU MUST BE

- a. Physically fit
- b. An expert on all possible debate topics
- c. Ready to fight dirty

10. DURING A DEBATE, YOU SHOULD REFRAIN FROM DOING HAND GESTURES THAT

- a. Could be construed as offensive
- b. Could cause an injury
- c. Could start a gang war

11. WHEN DEALING WITH THE MEDIA, YOU SHOULD *NOT*

- a. Work with your Communications Director to craft a narrative for your campaign
- b. Prepare for the press to report on everything you do
- c. Tell them to piss off

ANSWERS: 1. any are correct; 2. b; 3. b, and occasionally d; 4. c; 5. b; 6. a; 7. c; 8. a; 9. b; 10. all are correct; 11. c

CHAPTER 3

APPEARING PRESIDENTIAL

57

ACTING THE PART

APPEARANCE IS EVERYTHING

Personal appearance matters more in politics than any other profession, with the exception of banking and dressing in drag. And by "appearance," I'm not just talking about the clothes you wear. No, no. You need to hold yourself with confidence in all aspects of your life—from posture to hygiene to footwear—or it could color your entire legacy.

Rather than wearing the fashion of the day, Zachary Taylor preferred to wear his old military uniform, which was ragged and threadbare. But that still doesn't seem as offensive as Woodrow Wilson, who may have led countries toward peace after World War I, but had epically bad teeth. And Benjamin Harrison's greatest mark on history is that a White House visitor once described him as having a handshake "like a wilted petunia." Don't be like Benjamin.

So, in this section, you'll learn how to look and act presidential—tools you can use on the campaign trail and on the job in the White House. And if you don't make it to the big gig, at least you can get a job in banking.

BABY KISSING

The tradition of kissing babies dates back to the first elections in our country. Of course, back then it was a much more dangerous act, considering consumption, scarlet fever, and swine flu were all running rampant and everyone knows infants are just germ factories.

Thankfully, the worst thing you could get from a baby nowadays is a hearty cold and/or a stinky diaper. So, in this helpful graphic we'll skip the pre- and post-personal hygiene techniques and just focus on the kissing part.

HOW TO KISS A BABY

STEP 1: IDENTIFY THE BABY

STEP 2: PICK UP THE BABY

STEP 3: KISS THE BABY ON THE CHEEK OR HEAD

STEP 4: RETURN THE BABY

NOTE: MAKE SURE YOU ARE HOLDING THE BABY RIGHT SIDE UP

OTHER BABY KISSING TIPS

★ DON'T SCARE THE BABY   ★ DON'T BURP THE BABY (IT WILL LIKELY PUKE ON YOU)

★ DON'T SHAKE THE BABY   ★ DON'T SAY THE BABY LOOKS LIKE GOLLUM

★ DON'T HAND THE BABY TO A STRANGER   ★ DON'T CHECK THE BABY'S DIAPER

HANDSHAKING

In the course of your campaign, you'll shake a lot of hands. And after you become president, you'll shake even more. Anecdotal data shows the act of shaking hands makes up 98 percent of a Commander-in-Chief's daily schedule. The other 2 percent is holding meetings about which hands you must shake*.

The perfect handshake balances firmness and movement to create a gesture that conveys trust, power, and camaraderie. No pressure, but a bad handshake will always lead to nuclear war.

Teddy Roosevelt once held the Guinness World Record for most handshakes (8,513) in a single day.

HOW TO SHAKE HANDS

★ HAVE A STEADY APPROACH

★ GRIP FIRMLY, MOVE UP AND DOWN

★ DO NOT GRAB WRISTS (YOU ARE NOT A GLADIATOR)

★ DO NOT THUMB WRESTLE

★ DO NOT COME IN TOO HOT (INJURIES MAY RESULT)

*Anecdotal data is wholly unreliable.

SIGNING A DOCUMENT

Signatures on government documents are a big deal in America. And I don't mean for the obvious reason that without a signature some documents are just words on paper. No, they are such a big deal that we named the act of signing something after someone who signed something: John Hancock. For those of you unfamiliar with this term, John Hancock was the president of Congress and therefore the first of fifty-six people who signed the Declaration of Independence in 1776 and, because his signature was so delightfully flamboyant, we now say "put your John Hancock here" when we want someone to sign something. It's one of the small ways in which we continue to tease England.

HOW TO SIGN A DOCUMENT

Your signature should give the impression of authority and confidence. Typically, signatures—no matter how messy—have relatively defined initials, meaning the first letters of the first and last name are easily decipherable. And though cursive is used for most signatures, some employ a blend of cursive and manuscript (aka print) known as D'Nealian. If you need further inspiration, try creating a mood board or Pinterest collection of famous signatures. Practice often until the act becomes second nature.

When you're ready, hold the pen steady and let your movements be fluid. Also, you should refrain from dotting any i's with hearts.

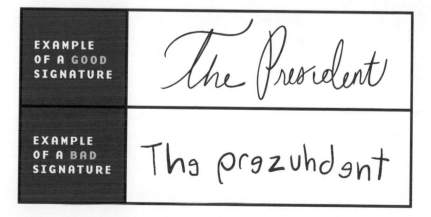

EXAMPLE OF A GOOD SIGNATURE	*The President*
EXAMPLE OF A BAD SIGNATURE	The przzuhdgnt

PRACTICE YOUR SIGNATURE

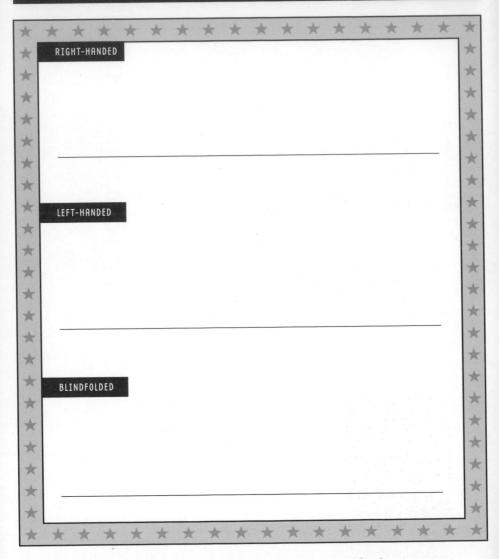

RIGHT-HANDED

LEFT-HANDED

BLINDFOLDED

Great. Now, let's work with a real government document. On the next page is an actual presidential proclamation originally signed by Herbert Hoover in 1931. You're going to sign it.

A PROCLAMATION

Proclamation 1974—Thanksgiving Day, 1931
November 3, 1931

By the President of the United States of America

We approach the season when, according to custom dating from the garnering of the first harvest by our forefathers in the New World, a day is set apart to give thanks even amid hardships to Almighty God for our temporal and spiritual blessings. It has become a hallowed tradition for the Chief Magistrate to proclaim annually a national day of thanksgiving.

Our country has cause for gratitude to the Almighty. We have been widely blessed with abundant harvests. We have been spared from pestilence and calamities. Our institutions have served the people. Knowledge has multiplied and our lives are enriched with its application. Education has advanced, the health of our people has increased. We have dwelt in peace with all men. The measure of passing adversity which has come upon us should deepen the spiritual life of the people, quicken their sympathies and spirit of sacrifice for others, and strengthen their courage. Many of our neighbors are in need from causes beyond their control and the compassion over this winter that they too may have full cause to participate in this day of gratitude to the Almighty.

Now, Therefore, I,   YOUR NAME HERE   , President of the United States of America, do hereby designate Thursday, November 26, 1931, as a National Day of Thanksgiving, and do recommend that our people rest from their daily labors and in their homes and accustomed places of worship give devout thanks for the blessings which a merciful Father has bestowed upon us.

In Witness Whereof, I have hereunto set my hand and caused the seal of the United States to be affixed.

Done at the City of Washington this 3rd day of November, in the year of our Lord nineteen hundred and thirty-one, and of the Independence of the United States of America the one hundred and fifty-sixth.

(sign here) _____

HOW TO WEAR A FLAG PIN

After the terrorist attacks of September 11, 2001, to represent our unity as a nation, President George W. Bush and members of his administration wore small American flag pins in their lapels. Since then, the pin has become a standard accessory for officials. In 2008, when then-candidate Barack Obama neglected to wear one, he was forced to explain himself during a debate with fellow candidate Hillary Clinton. The whole thing made headlines (and not the good kind). Needless to say, you don't want to mess this up.

OTHER TIPS FOR WEARING A FLAG PIN

★ DO NOT use a pin so small no one will see it

★ DO NOT wear the pin upside down

★ DO NOT use a Confederate flag pin

★ DO NOT use the pin to pick your teeth

SPEECH TECHNIQUES

TALKING THE TALK

Presidential politics claims some of the greatest moments in oratory artistry —from Franklin D. Roosevelt's 1933 inaugural address in which he said, "Let me assert my firm belief that the only thing we have to fear is fear itself," to Ronald Reagan's 1987 speech just feet from the Berlin Wall in which he boldly challenged the Soviet General Secretary with, "Mr. Gorbachev, tear down this wall." Of course, it also claims some of the worst moments, too. (We'll cover those later in the book.)

Your speech writers will play a key role in whether you are credited with a rousing and inspiring soliloquy on the future of our country or pundits add an "ism" to your name to define idiotic sayings. But we're focused on you right now, not the writers. So, let's limber up with some rhymes and tongue twisters.

VOCAL EXERCISES

Repeat the following tongue-twisting phrases aloud in front of the mirror each day and again before any public speaking engagement or debate.

- ★ *Washington crosses the Delaware sporting wooden teeth and whitish hair.*

- ★ *Jefferson's bud Hefferson Hudd told his old friend he wasn't a stud, but Jefferson thought he very much was, and now his legacy's mud.*

- ★ *Bush bet big on being better by dinner but bent and barfed on Japan's prime minister.*

- ★ *Zachary Taylor died of the toots. They buried him quick with his butt in his boots.*

WHAT TO DO WITH YOUR HANDS

For your hands, it's best to keep it basic. Don't go for any grandiose gestures. Leave that to the person on the side of the stage translating for the hearing impaired.

Throughout American history, there have been some pretty iconic political hand gestures. Nixon famously flashed a *V* with his index and third fingers quite often, even when leaving the office amid scandal, which is strange considering at the time the gesture meant "victory." Nelson Rockefeller, who briefly served as vice president under Gerald Ford, once flipped off a group of protesters, which probably explains why he was dropped from the ticket for the next election. And Donald Trump employed so many hand gestures—from one that looks as though he's holding a tiny potato chip to a repeated semi-clapping gesture meme makers call "the imaginary accordion"—that the rare speeches during which he refrained from moving gave everyone the heebie-jeebies.

In general, there are a handful of common gestures that fall into what is considered either acceptable or unacceptable categories. So here are a few examples of each.

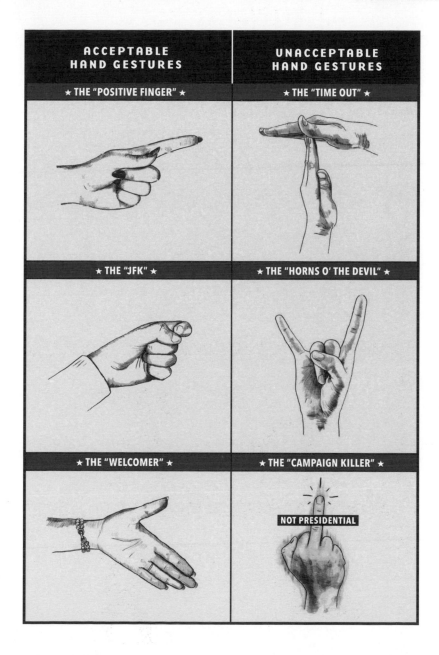

KEEPING IT CLASSY

WTF? MOMENTS

As history shows us, literally anything can happen to a candidate or president. Bob Dole's run for the highest office in the land fell apart after he toppled from a stage at a campaign event. Bill Clinton once fell asleep on live TV during a memorial for Martin Luther King, Jr.

One extreme WTF?! moment occurred during a press conference in Iraq when a journalist hurled his shoes at George W. Bush. Thanks to sharp reflexes and poor aerodynamics, the president was able to dodge the flying footwear. And that's the next lesson: be prepared for anything.

To cover all of the innumerable things that could possibly happen to you, let's focus on a few examples from the aforementioned Bush, Clinton, and Dole, as well as President Gerald Ford, whose falls were so common, they became a running gag on *Saturday Night Live*.

TECHNIQUES FOR PRETENDING YOU WEREN'T ASLEEP

WHEN YOUR HEAD BOB WAKES YOU, NOD IN SUDDEN AGREEMENT	PRETEND TO PICK SOME LINT FROM YOUR SUIT	COUGH (THIS WORKS TO COVER MANY GAFFES, INCLUDING FARTS)

FALL- AND/OR TRIP-RECOVERY TECHNIQUES

TRANSITION TO A QUICK TROT, AS IF EAGER TO GET TO YOUR DESTINATION

PRETEND TO SEE A COOL BUG OR FLOWER

BREAK INTO A DANCE STEP

DRESS FOR THE JOB

Some of our leaders made bold fashion moves, like John Quincy Adams, who reportedly was the first president to ditch the breeches and stockings worn by the founding fathers in favor of trousers, or John Tyler who rocked a large, floppy bowtie decades before it was considered in vogue. Others kept it classy, like John F. Kennedy, who preferred a slim, single-breasted suit. And some even changed fashion as we know it, such as Dwight D. Eisenhower, who as an Army General designed his own short military uniform jacket that was then adopted by the entire Army.

As you've undoubtedly heard on various fashion competition reality shows, the clothes make the man…Or woman…The clothes make the person or however you identify! (See "How Do You Identify," page 18.) But what person are you making? Here are a few inspirational collages that can help you find out what kind of president you want to be.

GET THE LOOK: CONSERVATIVE

"Conservative" doesn't mean republican, but rather someone who favors formal touches and modesty. Gray, navy blue, and black are solid bets. (You might notice a pattern starting with these three colors. That's because when Barack Obama dared to wear a beige suit once, the country totally freaked out.)

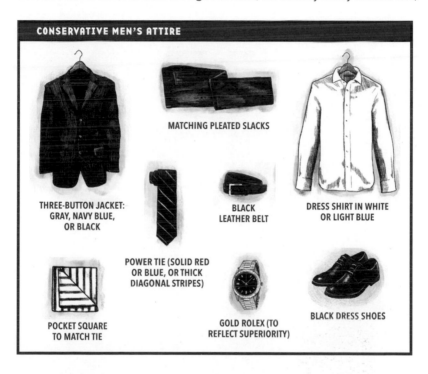

CONSERVATIVE MEN'S ATTIRE

MATCHING PLEATED SLACKS

THREE-BUTTON JACKET: GRAY, NAVY BLUE, OR BLACK

BLACK LEATHER BELT

DRESS SHIRT IN WHITE OR LIGHT BLUE

POWER TIE (SOLID RED OR BLUE, OR THICK DIAGONAL STRIPES)

POCKET SQUARE TO MATCH TIE

GOLD ROLEX (TO REFLECT SUPERIORITY)

BLACK DRESS SHOES

CONSERVATIVE WOMEN'S ATTIRE

TAILORED JACKET IN A SOLID COLOR, NO PATTERNS
MATCHING BELOW-THE-KNEE SKIRT
FITTED DRESS SHIRT
MODEST DIAMOND STUD EARRINGS
HIGH-HEEL SHOES
HOMESPUN SASS AND GRIT

GET THE LOOK: LIBERAL

As with the conservative looks, "liberal" doesn't mean Democrat. Oh, who am I kidding? Yes, it does. Just make sure you don't look like a New England college professor. No one wants to relive their Emily Brontë, model of modern romanticism literature class—so no elbow patches.

LIBERAL MEN'S ATTIRE
SINGLE-BREASTED JACKET: GRAY, NAVY BLUE, OR BLACK
MATCHING FLAT-FRONT SLACKS WHEN STUMPING ON THE CAMPAIGN TRAIL; "COOL" DAD JEANS FOR "CANDID" PHOTO OPS
DRESS SHIRT IN WHITE OR LIGHT BLUE
LOAFERS
LEATHER BELT (BLACK OR BROWN)
ANALOG WATCH
BASKETBALL FOR PICKUP GAMES WITH YOUR STAFF

LIBERAL WOMEN'S ATTIRE

SEXUAL HARASSMENT DEFLECTION HANDBOOK

FITTED DRESS SHIRT IN WHITE, JUST WHITE

FITTED JACKET IN BLACK, JUST BLACK

JIMMY CHOO HEELED SHOES

MATCHING TAPERED SLACKS

SMALL PENDANT NECKLACE

SLIGHTLY DANGLY EARRINGS

GET THE LOOK: INDEPENDENT

As previously addressed, there's actually an entire spectrum of ideologies that all tend to fall into the blanket category of "Independent." While you would naturally think those that fall into this category can dress in anything they want, up to and including a daring pith helmet and grass skirt combo, you'd be wrong. Remember, you're running for President of the United States, not president of the North County Wiccan Potluck Committee.

INDEPENDENT MEN'S ATTIRE

OFF-THE-RACK COTTON
DRESS SHIRT

PLEATED DOCKERS™
SLACKS

SNEAKERS (IN MUTED
TONES, NO NEON)

MID-LENGTH ALL-WEATHER
JACKET WITH POCKETS
FULL OF NOTES FROM
YOUR CAMPAIGN STAFF

WOVEN-HEMP BELT

IWATCH

INDEPENDENT WOMEN'S ATTIRE

SENSIBLE BUTTON-UP SHIRT
BLACK SKIRT, CUT JUST ABOVE THE KNEE
KITTEN-HEEL SHOES
SIMPLE HOOP EARRINGS
SIMPLE CHAIN NECKLACE, NO PENDANT
LIST OF QUOTABLE CATCH PHRASES

LET'S REVIEW

PRESIDENTIAL APPEARANCE TEST

Now that you've read the basics on how to look like you deserve the job, let's see how well you've retained it all. And keep in mind, it wasn't long ago that removing your suit jacket and rolling up your shirtsleeves were unheard of. Now, it's a go-to move to show you're just like one of the blue-collar folks out there in the heartland. So, if you miss a few of these, it's OK.

FILL IN ALL OVALS THAT APPLY

1. WHAT SHOULD YOU NOT DO WHEN KISSING A BABY?

○ a. Smile

○ b. Hand the baby back to the parent

○ c. Hand the baby to a stranger

2. WHAT IS ONE OF THE COMPONENTS OF A GOOD HANDSHAKE?

○ a. Thumb wrestling

○ b. Firm grip

○ c. Finger guns

3. YOUR SIGNATURE SHOULD SHOWCASE

○ a. Authority and confidence

○ b. Your best crayon colors

○ c. A naughty limerick

4. WHICH PROCLAMATION DID YOU SIGN?

○ a. Proclamation 1479

○ b. Proclamation 1974

○ c. What's a proclamation?

5. WHO ONCE MADE HEADLINES FOR NOT WEARING A FLAG PIN?

- ⬭ a. George W. Bush
- ⬭ b. Hillary Clinton
- ⬭ c. Barak Obama

6. WHICH OF THE FOLLOWING IS AN ACCEPTABLE HAND GESTURE?

- ⬭ a. The Welcomer
- ⬭ b. The Horns o' the Devil
- ⬭ c. The Time Out

7. TO AVOID EMBARRASSING MOMENTS, YOU SHOULD

- ⬭ a. Wear a mask
- ⬭ b. Try to fart backstage before you give a speech
- ⬭ c. Be prepared for anything

8. WHEN IS IT ACCEPTABLE TO CAMPAIGN IN A PITH HELMET AND GRASS SKIRT?

- ⬭ a. Always
- ⬭ b. Never
- ⬭ c. When running for president of the North County Wiccan Potluck Committee

CHAPTER 4

HOW GOVERNMENTING (AND PRESIDENTING) WORKS

[YOUR
FACE
HERE]

THE BASICS

BRANCHES AREN'T JUST FOR TREES

At this point, you should have all the information you need to prove your eligibility, build your campaign team, sort out your sartorial style, and pretty much everything else to get you to the White House. Because you're super optimistic, it's time to prepare for actually being there.

While it's not a necessity, you should have a working knowledge of how America keeps running. And since *West Wing* is no longer on the air, a thorough skimming of this chapter should totally get you up to speed. Let's start with the top-down view of the three branches of our government: judicial, legislative, and executive.

The idea of governing by these three branches was inspired by the writings of Montesquieu, a French philosopher, and tweaked for our country's purposes by James Madison in his Federalist Papers. The important thing to note here is that knowing this will make you look smart if you bring it up at a party.

The system was put in place by our founding fathers and defined in the Constitution to keep the power out of the hands of a single entity. The whole thing operates using a stalwart mechanism of checks and balances, blah, blah, blah. Basically, any big moves one branch wants to make has to be approved by one of the other branches. That's what all of that means.

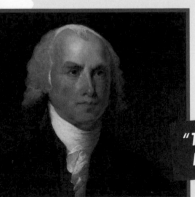

Sounds simple, right? Oh, man, it is such a mess. Don't get us wrong, it's our mess and it's important. This is a lovely mess of a republic, but it's a mess.

OK. Let's get down into it.

> *"THE TRUTH IS THAT ALL MEN HAVING POWER OUGHT TO BE MISTRUSTED."*
>
> — PRESIDENT JAMES MADISON

THE LEGISLATIVE BRANCH

The word "legislative" comes from the Latin root lex, which means "law" or, to use the more modern parlance, "hopelessly inefficient." This branch contains the House of Representatives and the Senate (AKA Congress). Every state has two senators, but the number of representatives is determined by each state's population. Basically, representatives speak for the people and senators speak for the state itself. This branch makes the laws. If the House and Senate are working on similar bills, they often try to meld them. If the president vetoes, Congress can override, but that's rare.

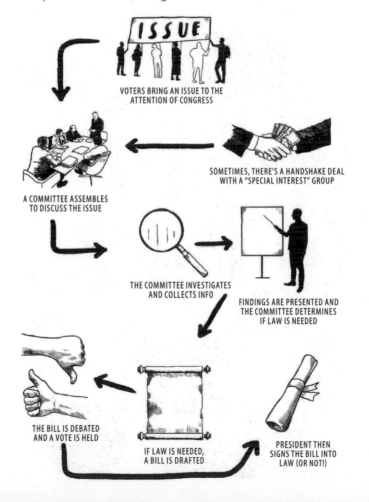

VOTERS BRING AN ISSUE TO THE ATTENTION OF CONGRESS

SOMETIMES, THERE'S A HANDSHAKE DEAL WITH A "SPECIAL INTEREST" GROUP

A COMMITTEE ASSEMBLES TO DISCUSS THE ISSUE

THE COMMITTEE INVESTIGATES AND COLLECTS INFO

FINDINGS ARE PRESENTED AND THE COMMITTEE DETERMINES IF LAW IS NEEDED

THE BILL IS DEBATED AND A VOTE IS HELD

IF LAW IS NEEDED, A BILL IS DRAFTED

PRESIDENT THEN SIGNS THE BILL INTO LAW (OR NOT!)

THE EXECUTIVE (THAT'S YOU!)

This is your time to shine. Just understand, it's not all about you, though going by the graph below, it sure looks like it is. But, no. The executive branch also includes the vice president, your cabinet, and, down the line, heads of various departments and enforcement agencies—those parts of government identified with three letters, like CIA, ATF, DEA, WTF, ETC... While the president (and vice president) are elected, most everyone else in this branch is appointed, though those must go through some rigorous scrutiny by the Senate. We'll get into exactly what you can do as president in a bit. For now, the broad stroke: this branch enforces the law.

THE JUDICIAL

The sole function of the judicial branch is to interpret the law. And when it comes to the other branches, this one is downright folksy in its simplicity. If you've seen even one show about a law firm, you know how this goes: a trial occurs. If the court rules against the defendant, they can appeal, and so on, until we get to the court named after a Taco Bell burrito. As with the legislative section, I'm skipping over some stuff, like the inner workings of state supreme courts and how, if the U.S. Supreme Court finds a law unconstitutional, that brings us back to the legislative branch. Anyway, that's it. Basically.

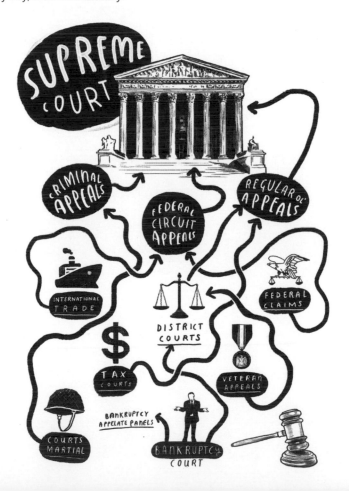

PREZ POWER

WHAT CAN A PRESIDENT DO?

The President of the United States is often described as the most powerful person in the world. This idea is rife with hyperbole. I mean, c'mon, power is relative. And though the president often serves as the most recognizable representative of our nation—which, let's face it, is pretty freaking awesome—there is someone who wields more power: the ~~Russian hacker~~ American voter.

Franklin D. Roosevelt once said, "The ultimate rulers of our democracy are not a president and senators and congressmen and government officials, but the voters of this country." That is still true today, despite politicians' seemingly endless attempts to ignore the will of the people and just do whatever the heck they want. You see, the key phrase there is "voters of this country." Even if those in various elected offices ignore the will of the people, the people can vote them out. All that is to say, the president has a lot of power, but don't go all Emperor Palpatine with it.

Those old white-haired dudes who wrote out the plan for our country centuries ago disagreed about a lot of things, like how much the president should actually be allowed to do. Some of them didn't want a president at all, others wanted the person in office to have very limited functionality. (They won out, by the way, hence the "checks and balances" thing.)

[Your name here] for president.

THINGS A PRESIDENT CAN DO WITHOUT APPROVAL

★ SIGN A BILL INTO LAW

★ VETO A BILL

★ SERVE AS COMMANDER-IN-CHIEF OF OUR MILITARY

★ SERVE AS OUR COUNTRY'S TOP DIPLOMAT

★ THROW A FEW WICKED PARTIES

★ MEET FAMOUS PEOPLE

★ PLAY FRISBEE IN THE SITUATION ROOM

★ TALK POLICY

★ NOMINATE PEOPLE FOR CERTAIN POSITIONS

★ SIGN EXECUTIVE ORDERS

★ HOST FOREIGN DIGNITARIES

★ GRANT FEDERAL PARDONS (TURKEY OR OTHERWISE)

That's it, really. Not much, right? Yet, watching the news, you'd think it was a lot more. That's because the power of the office has grown over the decades, but by how much and what that means is not always clearly defined. So, let's get into the gray area.

NAVIGATING (AROUND) PRESIDENTIAL LIMITATIONS

Nowadays, the big cheese in the White House has much more sway and influence over government affairs than was ever intended. But laws still exist to keep those powers in check as much as possible and to break those laws would be…well, against the law.

The exact limits of presidential powers are actually fairly easy to define: He or she (or they) can't do anything the other branches are supposed to do. But there are ways around some of those restrictions.

HOW TO GET AWAY WITH IT

★ MAKE BACKROOM DEALS

★ APPOINT PEOPLE WHO WILL CARRY OUT YOUR BIDDING

★ GO TO THE PRESS

★ MAKE PUBLIC DEALS

★ YOUR OLD FRIEND SUPER PAC

This sort of shady, double-dealing stuff happens all the time (which makes it totally OK, right?). Just be careful (especially with that Super PAC business), because getting caught is gonna buy you permanent residence at the Nixon Hotel or, worse, the Graybar Hotel. Or even worse, CNN's green room.

OTHER STUFF YOU CAN DO

The job of president isn't all chaos and disorder. There are also large amounts of confusion and mayhem.

I was going to say "just kidding," but I'd be just kidding about that. #prezlyfe is pretty much madness. Why would anyone want this job…?

Anyway, you do get to do a lot of cool crap too, like invite your favorite musician to come hang at the White House or tray surf down the aisle of the Air Force One during takeoff. Plus, people all over the world want to know what you have to say about literally anything. You could hold a press conference just to mention you finally binge-watched *The Americans*.

But do be aware that the press and the public will scrutinize every single word you say. Every. Single. Dang. Word. And probably every syllable as well. And you can't really go back and apologize for saying something you didn't mean because whatever you said that pissed everyone off will be what gets turned into a trending hashtag. So, try really hard not to say anything for which you'll need to apologize for. Or revisit. Or translate. Or fix. Or explain. And so on and so forth and whatnot.

"A PLEASANT TIME WAS NOT HAD BY ALL."

—NEW YORK POST REPORTER EDWARD LOWRY ON PRESIDENT WOODROW WILSON'S FIRST PRESS CONFERENCE

ANYONE CAN BE PRESIDENT

TIME TO TALK TURKEY

WATCH YOUR MOUTH

Naturally, you'll need to think carefully about word choice—what to say and what to avoid. We'll cover that in a sec. First, there are some situations you should be aware of before you start talking gibberish and make a total a-hole of yourself. It's bound to happen at some point, but let's try to minimize the level of "hole" when it does.

THE HOT MIC

"Hot" or "on and recording" microphones don't care if you say something stupid. They're just there, always listening.

THE GOTCHA QUESTION

These are questions meant to create a shocking moment or confession. Usually this is done when the interviewer asks a question that reveals they have more information than you thought.

THE TONGUE TWISTER

These generally occur when holding press conferences or press splashes with foreign dignitaries. For example, the current prime minister of Kazakhastan is Bakhytzhan Sagintayev. Give that a whirl with no warm up and see how you do.

THE LEADING QUESTION

Some reporters frame questions to entice a specific answer. Don't fall for it!

THE GAFFE

Accidentally saying the wrong country name or dignitary title, letting a cuss word or state secret slip—these types of things qualify as a gaffe. Obviously, there are degrees of severity.

THE INSENSITIVE COMMENT

The mother of all insensitive comments, "Let them eat cake," is (falsely) credited with kicking off the French Revolution. So, y'know, don't be a jerk.

86

SAY WHAT NOW?

Word choice. It's important. It's so important you might say it's very important. Based on presidential speeches from the past two decades, here's a super scientific and not-at-all made-up list of words to avoid.

WORDS AND PHRASES TO AVOID

- ★ ENTITLEMENT
- ★ HANDOUT
- ★ AID
- ★ WE'RE ALL GONNA DIE
- ★ OOPS
- ★ DOMESTIC TERROR
- ★ IMMIGRANT
- ★ MY RIDE-OR-DIE BESTIE PUTIN
- ★ IMAGINARY FRIEND
- ★ TIJUANA SEX SHOW
- ★ TAXES
- ★ EQUALITY
- ★ BUTT (SINGULAR)
- ★ BUTTS (PLURAL)

- ★ SATAN
- ★ TRAINS RUNNING ON TIME
- ★ OH, [INSERT PROFANITY HERE]
- ★ URBAN (EVERYONE KNOWS YOU MEAN BLACK)
- ★ WHO AM I AGAIN?
- ★ 9/11 WAS AN INSIDE JOB
- ★ BOMBING A COUNTRY (IN JEST)
- ★ BOMBING A COUNTRY (FOR REALS)
- ★ WEINER (OR ANY OTHER NAUGHTY BODY PART)
- ★ HOOTERS (EVEN IN REFERENCE TO THE BAR)
- ★ ABORTION
- ★ FORD'S THEATRE
- ★ WHAT YOU CAN DO FOR YOUR COUNTRY
- ★ SCREW WHITE PRIVILEGE

This would be a perfect place to provide a list of words that are generally acceptable, but I already did that in the section on creating your campaign slogan. Just go back to that page, grab a smattering of those words, add some conjunctions or whatever to make them sound like sentences, and you've got yourself an uplifting speech.

POWER PLAYS

TEE TIME

One of the many perks of sitting in the Oval Office is spending your weekends sitting in a golf cart. William Howard Taft started the tradition of presidents hitting the fairway, and only three since have not golfed—Jimmy Carter, Herbert Hoover, and Harry S. Truman. Some Commanders-in-Chief use the pastime to hold casual meetings with friends and foes. Others use it simply to get away from the duties of the job for a few hours. Whatever the reason, spending a morning on the links affords you the opportunity to clear your head and replace it with rage that you can't fix your slice. But you can fill it with something else: presidential pondering.

Just as with your speech, the frequency of visits to the golf course—as well as your swing, club choice, score, chip shots, attire, drive power, short game—will be subject to scrutiny by the press and the public. Coming off the eighteenth hole, you'll likely see at least a few members of the media. When approached, let them know you were considering national and global events.

It may be total bull, but it will stop them from simply reporting how much you golf, which in recent years has become increasingly unfashionable. To assist you in this ~~ruse~~ effort, here's an informative list on merging golf with political meditations.

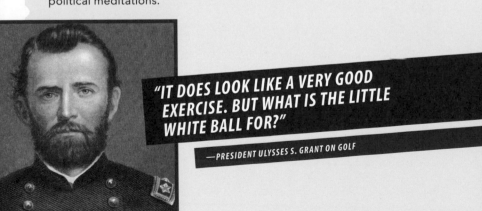

"IT DOES LOOK LIKE A VERY GOOD EXERCISE. BUT WHAT IS THE LITTLE WHITE BALL FOR?"

—PRESIDENT ULYSSES S. GRANT ON GOLF

THE POLITICS OF GOLFING

1A. KEEP A WIDE STANCE AND BRING YOUR ELBOWS UP EVENLY

1B. FOLLOW THROUGH AS YOU WOULD DURING NUCLEAR DE-ESCALATION TALKS WITH NORTH KOREA

2A. PLACE A FOOT HIGH ON THE TRAP, AND PIVOT YOUR WRISTS

2B. SNAP YOUR CLUB IN A SHORT ARC TO RAISE THE BAIL UP LIKE THE NATIONAL EMPLOYMENT RATE

3A. LEAD WITH YOUR FRONT FOOT, AND YOU'LL HAVE A DIAGONAL SWING

3B. KEEP YOUR FOOT LINE STRAIGHT LIKE YOU STAND FIRM ON COAL

4A. FOOT PLACEMENT IS CRITICAL. YOUR BACK HEAL SLIGHTLY BEHIND YOUR FRONT GIVES YOU A CONTROLLED FADE

4B. WITH YOUR FRONT HEEL SLIGHTLY BEHIND, YOU'LL GET A CONTROLLED DRAW, SENDING THE BALL AROUND HAZARDS JUST AS YOU SENT THAT ECONOMIC PACKAGE BACK TO CONGRESS

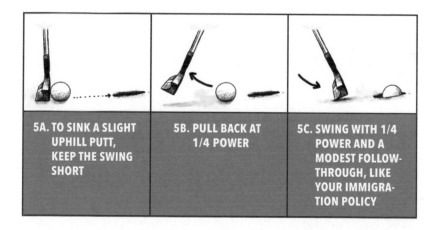

5A. TO SINK A SLIGHT UPHILL PUTT, KEEP THE SWING SHORT

5B. PULL BACK AT 1/4 POWER

5C. SWING WITH 1/4 POWER AND A MODEST FOLLOW-THROUGH, LIKE YOUR IMMIGRATION POLICY

THE FIRST PRESIDENTIAL IMPEACHMENT

Though we are a nation of laws, the only reason we have the judicial branch is to navigate the gray areas between, on top of, next to, and under them. And sometimes presidents explore those gray areas on their own and get gray all over them. That's why we have the impeachment process, which allows for criminal (and non-criminal) charges to be brought against a sitting politician. If convicted, the process then allows for that person to be removed from office. That's important—it's a two-step process.

As of this writing, only two presidents in history have ever been impeached. I say "as of this writing" because no matter who sits in the Oval Office, some group always calls for impeachment. It's just a thing that happens. On that note: should you make it to the White House, enjoy your attempted impeachment.

Andrew Johnson, our seventeenth president, got the coveted gig of Commander-in-Chief after the assassination of Abraham Lincoln. This was back when Democrats in the South were still pro-slavery. Not really a bright spot in that party's history. After they got their asses handed to them in the Civil War, Abe wanted to get the country back to hugging and high-fiving status, so he picked Johnson, a Democrat, as his vice president and the yin to his republican yang. But, then John Wilkes Booth got all trigger happy, Johnson became president, and the Republican-controlled Congress found, to their horror, they had to deal with a Democrat in the White House.

"EXPERIENCE HAS ALREADY SHOWN THAT THE IMPEACHMENT THE CONSTITUTION HAS PROVIDED IS NOT EVEN A SCARECROW."

—PRESIDENT THOMAS JEFFERSON

"IT DEPENDS UPON WHAT THE MEANING OF THE WORD 'IS' IS."

—PRESIDENT BILL CLINTON IN GRAND JURY TESTIMONY DEFENDING HIS STATEMENT "THERE'S NOTHING GOING ON BETWEEN US" IN REGARD TO HIS AFFAIR WITH A WHITE HOUSE INTERN

Johnson embarked on a speaking tour during which he basically talked trash about Republicans, and they saw the proverbial writing on the proverbial wall. So, they quickly passed the Tenure of Office Act, which prohibited the president from firing cabinet members without Senate approval. That may seem like a dick move, but keep in mind Johnson was opposed to equal rights for black people and an all-around schmuck (reportedly, he was too drunk to show up for his and Lincoln's inauguration). And it appears he wasn't the smartest suit in the closet either because, even after the passage of the Tenure of Office Act, he went ahead and fired the Secretary of War Edwin Stanton, with whom he'd often clashed.

Congress thought, "We got that S.O.B.!" and voted to impeach him (with a House vote of 126 to 47 in favor). When time came to actually put him on trial and hopefully kick him out of office, things didn't go so smoothly. That's the problem with hastily written laws—they're full of vague language open to interpretation. With a Senate vote of 35 not guilty to 19 guilty votes, Johnson walked freely back into the White House, undoubtedly tossing up double middle fingers as he did so.

The second presidential impeachment occurred because Bill Clinton let his dingle dangle where he shouldn't have and then lied about it. That's an important distinction—he didn't break the law by messing around with an intern, he broke the law by lying about messing around with an intern. The official charges were perjury and obstruction of justice. Like Johnson, the Senate acquitted him and, in the end, the only casualty was the definition of the word "is."

Oh, and contrary to what you may think, Nixon was never officially impeached. The House started the procedure, but ol' Tricky Dick resigned before it got to that.

LET'S GET BUSY

A DAY IN THE LIFE OF A PRESIDENT

Earlier in this book, I stated that 98 percent of a president's day was shaking hands. Sorry, but if you believed that I have a bridge to sell you, and it's called peace in the Middle East. Here's a sample schedule for one day:

MORNING	
4:00 AM	Wake. Get update on ISIS movements during the night.
4:15 AM	Morning security briefing.
5:45 AM	Breakfast.
5:50 AM	Update from Chief of Staff on the day's schedule.
5:55 AM	Call with British prime minister regarding sanctions on North Korea.
6:10 AM	Meeting with the Joint Chiefs of Staff regarding a terrorist attack in France.
6:30 AM	Mid-morning screaming break.
6:35 AM	Go over speech for the senatorial campaign appearance you agreed to do.
6:45 AM	Stress eat a whole sleeve of Oreos.
6:50 AM	Photo op with representative from South Dakota's 33rd district and her whiny kids.
7:00 AM	Meeting with senior staff to discuss immigration reform.
7:30 AM	Complain to Chief of Staff that you picked immigration reform as a signature issue.
7:40 AM	More screaming, just at the wall or something.
7:45 AM	Update on the situation in France.
8:15 AM	Address complaint from kitchen staff that someone keeps eating all of the Oreos.
8:20 AM	Call with French president.
8:30 AM	Apologize to French president for joke about baguette sticking out of shopping bag.
8:45 AM	Briefing on the new infrastructure initiative you don't remember announcing.
9:00 AM	Information gathering meeting with economic advisors on global trade.
10:30 AM	Second breakfast.
10:40 AM	Brush teeth and shower (because there wasn't time when you woke up).

MIDDAY	
11:00 AM	Staff informs you of a train derailment in Oregon.
11:15 AM	Press briefing about the French terror attack, North Korean sanctions, the new infrastructure initiative, and the train derailment in Oregon.
12:00 PM	Meeting with representatives from local law enforcement and drug treatment centers to discuss the opioid-addiction epidemic.
12:45 PM	Emergency meeting with the Homeland Security deputy director to discuss possible terror attack in West Virginia.
1:00 PM	Meeting with representatives of DHS, CIA, and FBI to track events in West Virginia.
1:20 PM	Group sigh of relief when the explosion in West Virginia turns out to be a coal mine cave-in.
1:21 PM	Realize the sigh of relief was insensitive, orders given to monitor situation.
1:22 PM	Lunch.
1:25 PM	Traveling in the motorcade, get briefed on North Korean leader, who just called you a buffoon.
2:00 PM	Read a storybook to kids at a local elementary school.
2:15 PM	Get a tour of the classroom from a teacher and the students.
2:30 PM	Photo op with the kids and announcement of your new education funding initiative.
2:45 PM	Traveling in the motorcade, told the North Korean leader just threatened to fire nuclear missiles, just to show they can.
3:15 PM	Back at the White House, update on West Virginia mine cave-in casualties (3), injuries (12), and trapped miners (2).
3:20 PM	Call with the mining company, offer to send assistance if needed.
3:25 PM	Literally, just staring at a chair and listening to the screaming in your brain for, like, five straight minutes.
3:30 PM	Emergency meeting with the Joint Chiefs in the Situation Room, ISIS commander located, you give the order to strike.
3:45 PM	Monitor the military drone strike on ISIS camp, commander killed.
4:30 PM	Calls to families of soldiers killed in action.

EVENING

5:00 PM	Welcome dignitaries from Algeria, including the prime minister.
5:30 PM	Closed-door meeting with Algerian prime minister about natural-gas exports to Europe and other countries.
6:00 PM	Press conference with Algerian prime minister about lowering tariffs on some imports.
6:30 PM	Meeting in Situation Room about North Korean nuclear threat, the aftermath of the terror attack in France, the follow-up on the strike on the ISIS camp.
7:00 PM	Dinner with Algerian dignitaries.
8:00 PM	Hide in a closet and eat another sleeve of Oreos.
8:10 PM	Communications director informs you of a protest at a courthouse in Arizona has turned violent.
8:15 PM	Meeting with Senate committee chair about strategic oil reserves and the possibility of drilling on federal land.
8:29 PM	Wave to vice president as you pass in the hall.
8:30 PM	Emergency meeting with CIA deputy director regarding new intel on ISIS, attack planned in London.
8:35 PM	Phone call with British prime minister regarding ISIS threat, assistance offered.
8:45 PM	Communications director informs you protest riot in Arizona has been quelled, the trapped West Virginia miners are free, and the train derailment has some fatalities.
8:50 PM	Stress eat family size bag of Cool Ranch Doritos.
8:52 PM	Read file of new intel on North Korean nuclear program.
9:00 PM	Watch old episode of *Project Runway*, just to unwind.
9:30 PM	Meeting in Situation Room about the ISIS threat in London, one operative captured, two others still at large.
9:45 PM	Chief of staff updates you on the train derailment—brakes failed, 3 casualties, 22 injured, Department of Transportation investigators are on scene.
9:50 PM	Staff rundown of tomorrow's schedule.
10:00 PM	Sit on the toilet and shake as you finish off the Oreos.

LET'S REVIEW

DECODE THE MESSAGE

For this quiz, you'll have to decipher a top-secret message given to you by a joint task force made up of members of the FBI and the Secret Service. You've been given five of the letters to get you started, but you must figure out the rest. Set a timer to see how fast you can decode the message. The clock is ticking. Go!

A	B	C	D	E	F	G	H	I	J	K	L	M	N	O	P	Q	R	S	T	U	V	W	X	Y	Z
		24		17			19				21									2					

_E_ _H_U_H_ _E_ _ECE___E_
22 17 12 19 23 2 18 19 12 22 17 1 17 24 17 11 20 17 5

_ _H___E_ _H_E__, _U_ __
4 7 19 23 13 17 12 19 1 17 4 12 10 2 12 11 12

___ _U___ _ ____C_LL_
22 4 9 16 2 9 12 4 1 23 10 23 24 4 21 21

_____E_____ _ ____E_H___E.
23 15 15 17 1 11 13 18 4 12 1 26 17 9 19 4 1 17

ANSWER: WE THOUGHT WE RECEIVED A PHONE THREAT, BUT IT WAS JUST A ROBOCALL OFFERING A TIMESHARE.

95

WHO OR WHICH PART DOES WHAT AND HOW?

By now, you have as full an understanding of how our government works as at least a third of our past presidents did. Let's review with a little quiz, shall we?

FILL IN ALL OVALS THAT APPLY

1. THE SOLE PURPOSE OF THE JUDICIAL BRANCH IS TO

- ◯ a. Interpret laws
- ◯ b. Make laws
- ◯ c. Break laws

2. THE EXECUTIVE BRANCH

- ◯ a. Is a new dance craze sweeping the nation
- ◯ b. Includes many cabinet members
- ◯ c. Is the biggest part of an oak tree

3. THE LEGISLATIVE BRANCH CAN

- ◯ a. Write laws, but not enforce them
- ◯ b. Bake cookies, but not eat them
- ◯ c. Take anyone they want to their country club

4. WHICH IS NOT A WAY A BILL BECOMES A LAW

- ◯ a. The president signs it
- ◯ b. Congress overrides a presidential veto
- ◯ c. It emerges from its cocoon

5. WHEN DETERMINING WHETHER A NEW LAW IS NEEDED, A COMMITTEE WILL OFTEN

- ◯ a. Check to see what's trending on Twitter
- ◯ b. Hold a poetry slam
- ◯ c. Assign a research team to collect information on the subject

ANSWERS: 1. a; 2. b; 3. a; 4. c; 5. c

FILL IN THE OVAL WITH THE CORRECT ANSWER

1. SOMETHING A PRESIDENT CAN'T DO IS HOST DIGNITARIES

- ◯ True
- ◯ False

2. A WAY AROUND LIMITATIONS OF PRESIDENTIAL POWER IS TO OFFER A BRIBE

- ◯ True
- ◯ False

3. IN SPEECHES, YOU SHOULD AVOID USING THE WORD "BUTTS"

- ◯ True
- ◯ False

4. THE PASTIME PLAYED BY MOST OF OUR FORMER PRESIDENTS IS SOCCER

- ◯ True
- ◯ False

5. THE FIRST U.S. PRESIDENT TO BE IMPEACHED WAS BILL CLINTON

- ◯ True
- ◯ False

6. A TYPICAL DAY IN THE LIFE OF A PRESIDENT HAS LOTS OF DOWNTIME

- ◯ True
- ◯ False

7. A "HOT MIC" MEANS AN ATTRACTIVE DEVICE USED TO RECORD SOUND

- ◯ True
- ◯ False

ANSWERS: 1. False; 2. False; 3. True; 4. False; 5. False; 6. False; 7. False

CHAPTER 5

YOU MADE IT!

NOW WHAT?

99

HAIL TO THE CHIEF!

A BIRD'S-EYE VIEW AND OTHER IMPORTANT STUFF

You and your team ran a great campaign, and voters swept you into office...
Well, technically, it was the electoral college that swept you into office.
That's because we have what's called an "indirect election" process in this
country. So, sure, citizens vote, but it's actually a relatively small group of
people who determine...You know what, let's just say it's complicated.
Now, where were we? Ah, yes.

Congratulations! The inauguration was a blast, and now it's time to get to
work. Before you go waltzing through the hallowed corridors of the White
House, there are a few more things you should know. Thank God, you have
this book.

You know who does what in D.C., but you need to know where they do it
and what it's like to work with them. This next section will teach you not just
how to work with your fellow politicians and other groups, but how to find
them. Plus, you'll get a run-through of a few particular scenarios a president
might encounter.

A BRIEF WORD ON FIRST LADIES

As of this writing, no woman has had the pleasure of welcoming her hubby into the White House as First Man or First Dude or whatever he'd be called. We look forward to a possible updated edition in the near future when we can remedy that.

In the meantime, it's time to honor the better half of some of our presidents. And by honor, we mean find really awesome stories and share them.

ABIGAIL ADAMS

The wife of John Adams was a huge proponent of women's equality. She constantly lobbied her husband to consider and/or include women in various official proceedings and famously wrote in a letter to him, "Remember, all men would be tyrants if they could." She was also the first woman to be a wife to one president and a mother to another. (The only other woman to do that was Barbara Bush.)

MARY TODD LINCOLN

Before her husband was assassinated, Mary lost her parents and two of her sons, which exacerbated what we now know was probably clinical depression. But, that didn't stop her from visiting and caring for horribly wounded soldiers and generally pissing off the press with her unusual clothes and extravagant parties.

ELEANOR ROOSEVELT

To be perfectly frank, Eleanor was a total badass. She had her own newspaper column and regular radio address in which she lobbied for equal rights and other then-taboo political ideals, much to the frustration of her hubby Franklin. She also refused Secret Service protection, preferring instead to carry a gun.

WHERE ARE WE?

Congress may write the laws that make the whole country sing, but they don't do it in one place. Senators and representatives hold debates and votes at the Capitol Building, but much of the work happens at separate offices. And there are just so darn many of those buggers (plus their staff) that the individual offices sit in six separate buildings around the Capitol Building.

As you'll learn, the White House is a bit of a hike from where most of the other lawmakers work. The good news is, because you are the headiest of honchos, anyone who needs to discuss anything with you will either call or just come to you. Generally, if the president shows up in the Capitol Building, it's either for the State of the Union address or something in the country has gone very, very wrong.

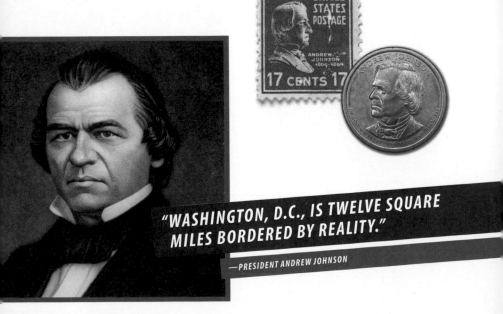

"WASHINGTON, D.C., IS TWELVE SQUARE MILES BORDERED BY REALITY."

—PRESIDENT ANDREW JOHNSON

Also, there are so many department buildings—Department of Commerce, Department of Energy, Department of Repetition Department, and so on— and so many intelligence agencies and other government-related offices, things can get really confusing really fast, so we're just going to focus on the legislative and judicial branch buildings. Oh, and you'll see where to get a good Bloody Mary at the Old Ebbitt Grill, which is where power players in D.C. go to talk deals and drink their lunch.

The layout of the city may seem to make little sense at first glance, but there's a method to the madness. And it's a French method. George Washington himself asked Pierre L'Enfant, a French architect who fought alongside us Americans in the Revolutionary War, to design the city. L'Enfant's plan was to have the capital resemble European cities like Paris. So, when you get lost among the dizzying diagonal intersections, feel free to shout, "Merde!"

Also, if you need to get somewhere not pictured (a likely scenario), you can ask someone and they'll tell you. It's likely in their job description.

D.C. HOT SPOTS

VIRGINIA

1.

MARYLAND

5.

6.

2.

3.

4.

7.

8.

1. WHITE HOUSE
(That's where you live.)

2. NATIONAL MALL
(Lots of dudes selling T-shirts, tourists, tons of pigeons, some hobos.)

3. HOUSE OFFICE BUILDINGS
(Where representatives hang pictures of their family.)

4. LIBRARY OF CONGRESS
(Overdue fees here likely include jail time.)

5. OLD EBBITT GRILL
(Where politicians make deals while eating burgers.)

6. HOTELS AND BARS AND STUFF
(Where politicians meet with "escorts" in a purely "platonic" way, like they're just making sure these escorts are keeping up with their "studies" so they can get that sociology degree.)

7. SENATE OFFICE BUILDINGS
(Where senators take ~~bribes~~ meetings.)

8. SUPREME COURT
(Like other courts, but more supreme.)

THE PRESIDENTIAL PETS

Pets make great companions and also have the effect of humanizing our nation's leader—even if they normally come off as an emotionless slab of granite. As far back as George Washington, who had a pack of hounds, animals have sat beside (or on) the person in the big chair. And though dogs can claim the title of most common presidential pet, there have been a few other beasts in the White House.

James Buchanan was reportedly gifted a herd of elephants by the King of Siam. He donated all but one to a zoo and kept the lone pachyderm on the White House grounds.

Looking for something smaller? Thomas Jefferson had a pet mockingbird named Dick. But he wasn't the only (or even first) bird to hang out with a president. George Washington's and James Madison's wives kept parrots around for, I don't know, maybe companionship? Being a presidential spouse can be quite lonely, after all.

Both Teddy Roosevelt and Calvin Coolidge are said to have had a literal zoo at the White House, each with numerous animals. And John Quincy Adams was rumored to have an alligator, a gift to him from the Marquis de Lafayette.

And that's not even getting into all of the cats, horses, sheep, cows, chickens that have set foot—or rather paw or hoof or whatever—on government ground.

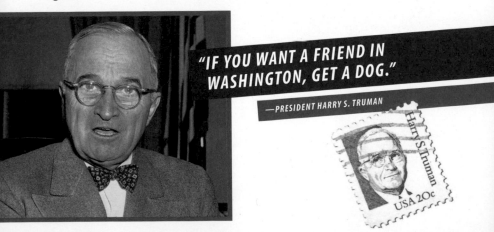

"IF YOU WANT A FRIEND IN WASHINGTON, GET A DOG."

—*PRESIDENT HARRY S. TRUMAN*

YOUR PRESIDENTIAL PET

Close your eyes and point to see which animal you should choose to make you seem more human by comparison.

SEE WHICH CRITTER YOU SHOULD HAVE IN THE WHITE HOUSE.

WORKING IT

OK, now wait. Did you know we have a president to thank for the term OK? Martin Van Buren, our eighth president and Dr. Emmet Brown lookalike, was raised in Kinderhook, NY, which earned him the nickname Old Kinderhook. At campaign events in 1840, his supporters adopted and chanted the initials O.K., which previously appeared in a couple of *Boston Morning Post* columns as a joke (it stood for "oll korrect," a purposeful misspelling of "all correct"), to imply Old Kinderhook is all correct. So, thanks to newspaper smartassery and a powerful yet unsuccessful re-election campaign, we now have two letters that mean "uh, yeah, sure."

Anyway, we already went over what a typical day is like, so now we're going to get into the messy gastrointestinal tract of government that turns your efforts into real turds…uh, results. We meant results.

On a daily basis, you'll have interactions with Congress, the press, foreign leaders, the public, your staff, probably an intelligence official or two, and maybe even a food delivery guy. Each of these interactions has its own etiquette. In other words, you gotta know how to converse and exchange information with a crapload of different personalities without starting a national crisis (unless, of course, that's your goal). OK? OK.

PROPER MEETING AND GREETING

We're not going to cover every single possible interaction, because that'd take hundreds of volumes and dozens of years to explain and, quite frankly, the country is already on a fast track to Hades, and we don't want you to have to read this book by the light of a nation in flames. So, what follows are a few ol' standbys to show you how it's done, and you can figure the rest out. You can figure out the rest, right? God help us otherwise.

DO

- ★ SHAKE HANDS
- ★ BE RESPECTFUL AND CHOOSE YOUR WORDS CAREFULLY
- ★ LISTEN TO ANY/ALL CONCERNS
- ★ MAINTAIN EYE CONTACT
- ★ STAY AWARE OF THE SCHEDULE
- ★ OFFER TO HEAR ALL OPTIONS
- ★ CONSIDER THE PERSON'S BACKGROUND
- ★ RELY ON YOUR ADVISORS
- ★ EDUCATE YOURSELF ON THE ISSUE
- ★ FIND COMMON GROUND
- ★ NEGOTIATE W/ GOOD FAITH
- ★ AGREE TO FOLLOW UP

DON'T

- ★ KISS ON THE MOUTH
- ★ REFUSE TO NEGOTIATE
- ★ SHOUT OVER PEOPLE TO BE HEARD
- ★ LEER
- ★ GET HIGH BEFOREHAND
- ★ ROLL YOUR EYES WHEN THEY LIST OPTIONS
- ★ MAKE FUN OF THE PERSON'S BACKGROUND
- ★ IGNORE THE DATA
- ★ GIVE THEM A NICKNAME ON THE SPOT
- ★ REFUSE TO BUDGE ON ISSUES
- ★ LIE
- ★ AGREE TO TEXT, BUT NEVER DO IT

HOW TO DEAL WITH FOREIGN DIGNITARIES

Your role as the face of our country means you will meet, host, and be the guest of leaders and government officials from all over the world. So, y'know, don't screw that up. Try the following quiz using terms and suggestions from the U.S. State Department's protocol guidelines and its very own Foreign Service Institute (a kind of training program for diplomats), and see if your instincts and knowledge can guide you through such an encounter.

FILL IN THE OVAL WITH THE CORRECT ANSWER

1. BEFORE WELCOMING A FOREIGN GUEST, YOU SHOULD
- a. Meet with a representative from the State Department or other diplomatic official
- b. Meet with your stylist
- c. Meet with a psychic

2. IN A PRIVATE MEETING WITH MORE THAN ONE REPRESENTATIVE FROM A SINGLE COUNTRY, THE HIGHEST-RANKED VISITOR SHOULD BE SEATED
- a. On the right side of the couch
- b. On the left side of the couch
- c. Next to the champagne fountain

3. AS PRESIDENT, YOU SHOULD EXIT THE MEETING WITH
- a. The best-dressed visitor
- b. The highest-ranked visitor
- c. A musical number

4. WHEN HOSTING A FOREIGN DIGNITARY AT AN EVENT IN THE US
- a. You should comment on their hair
- b. Traditional American food should be served
- c. The visitor's national anthem should be played before that of the US

5. WHEN DISPLAYING FLAGS DURING A FOREIGN DIGNITARY'S VISIT, THEIR FLAG
- a. Should be flown on the same staff as the US flag
- b. Should be flown to the viewer's left
- c. Should be worn as a cape

6. WHEN A GUEST OF THE PRESIDENT, VISITING DIGNITARIES STAY

- ○ a. At a Motel 6
- ○ b. At the Pentagon
- ○ c. At the Blair House

7. WHEN VISITING THE US, WHO GETS PROTECTION FROM THE STATE DEPARTMENT'S DIPLOMACY SECURITY SERVICE (AS OPPOSED TO THE SECRET SERVICE)

- ○ a. A foreign minister
- ○ b. A head of government
- ○ c. ALF

8. ACCORDING TO U.S. DIPLOMATIC PROTOCOL, WHICH ARE THE 2 ACCEPTABLE STYLES OF EATING

- ○ a. Paleo and flexitarian
- ○ b. American and Continental
- ○ c. American and French

9. BEFORE PLANNING A MEAL, YOUR TEAM SHOULD

- ○ a. Familiarize themselves with dietary, cultural, and religious restrictions
- ○ b. Stock up on butter
- ○ c. Get some delivery menus

RESULTS

IF YOU GOT ALL 9 CORRECT, YOU ARE READY TO REPRESENT OUR COUNTRY.

IF YOU GOT 5 OR MORE ANSWERS CORRECT, YOU SHOULD REVIEW U.S. DIPLOMATIC PROTOCOLS.

IF YOU GOT 4 OR FEWER ANSWERS CORRECT, YOU SHOULD HIRE A STELLAR SECRETARY OF STATE.

ANSWERS: 1. a; 2. a; 3. b; 4. c; 5. b; 6. c; 7. a; 8. b; 9. a

HOW TO DEAL WITH THE PRESS

A common term for the press and the media in America is the "Fourth Estate," because, though it isn't an official branch of the government, it's just as important and often just as powerful. What to say and what to not say when campaigning has already been laid out, more or less. Now that you're in the White House, there's more to know, y'know?

There's a whole group of reporters whose sole job is to report on everything you do—the White House Press Corp. (or the White House Press Pool). Your Communications Director and Press Secretary will usually handle them, but they're still asking questions about you the whole time and sometimes you'll go up to that podium and take them on yourself. And know that if things start spinning out of control, you cannot hit a button to open the floor in the White House press room and send the press pool into the actual pool beneath. That pool is empty.

★ DO MEMORIZE EACH REPORTER'S NAME

★ DO STAY ON POINT, EVEN WHEN A REPORTER ATTEMPTS TO LEAD YOU TO ANOTHER TOPIC

★ DON'T LIE (REPORTERS *ALWAYS* FIND OUT THE TRUTH)

★ DON'T SHOW UP TO A PRESS EVENT DRUNK

PRESIDENTIAL SLIPUPS

No matter how hard you try, you can't present flawless speech or remember every bit of diplomatic formality every time you get up in front of a crowd or step foot in another country. You'll slip up once in a while. But, don't worry. You won't be the first. Speech and etiquette gaffes are a part of every presidency.

George W. Bush held the office of president during the worst terrorist attack in U.S. history and that will undoubtedly be his legacy. But before then (and a bit after really), he had a reputation for bungling speeches and…well, the English language, in general. Once of his most memorable garbled moments came during a speech in Nashville a year after the tragic events of Sept. 11, 2001. He tripped over a simple colloquialism, saying, "Fool me once, shame on…shame on you. Fool me…you can't get fooled again." Not exactly the rousing words of a stalwart leader. Nor was the time in 2004 when he said, "[Our enemies] never stop thinking about new ways to harm our country and our people, and neither do we."

Look, Bush's vocal and physical mistakes are so numerous, that I could dedicate a whole section of this book to cataloging them—that's why the term "Bushism" came to describe his unique mangling of his own diction—but let's move on.

Jimmy Carter once accidentally said he wanted to bone an entire country. Thanks to the mistake of a translator, part of his 1977 speech to residents in Warsaw in which he said, "I have come to learn your opinions and understand your desire for the future," was translated as, "I desire the Poles

carnally." Hubba hubba, Jimmy. It doesn't help the former peanut farmer's image that, a year earlier, he made sexy news when he admitted in a *Playboy* profile, "I've looked on a lot of women with lust. I've committed adultery in my heart many times." That's not necessarily a slip of the tongue but rather a terribly bad time and place to admit something like that.

At least he didn't insult physically or mentally challenged individuals. During a 2009 appearance on *The Tonight Show*, Barack Obama said this of his bowling game: "It's like...It was like Special Olympics or something." Not cool, Obama. Not cool.

Like a touring rock star, sometimes all of the cities and countries you visit blur together. Maybe that explains Ronald Reagan's mental state while the guest of one particular foreign leader. During a fancy banquet, Reagan raised his glass and toasted "the people of Bolivia." Unfortunately, he was in Brazil.

There is some debate as to whether everyone's favorite presidential speech gaffe actually happened. In 1963, John F. Kennedy gave an anticommunist speech in West Berlin to show support to Germany in the wake of the construction of the Berlin Wall. While it is considered one of the best of such addresses ever delivered, it seems Kennedy's strong Boston accent and his possible mispronunciation of the word "Berliner" caused some to believe his declaration "Ich bin ein Berliner!" ("I am a Berliner!") was actually the declaration "I am a jelly donut!" Whether true or not, go ahead and consider yourself a patriot every time you eat a jam-filled pastry.

CRISIS MANAGEMENT

HOW TO DEAL

There will likely come a time in your presidency when you will be called upon to see our country through a national crisis. While you'll have the full force and resources of the entire United States government and/or military behind you, you are the person the citizens will turn to for comfort and security. When this happens, you'll feel the crushing weight of responsibility for the hundreds of millions of American people, of our proud history, of your own legacy, and for the national supply of Ben & Jerry's Chubby Hubby ice cream everyone will undoubtedly stress eat. This is not a time to panic.

This moment will be the one for which history judges and lionizes you. Think of the bombing of Pearl Harbor. It was a terrible event and the country was scared. But Franklin D. Roosevelt roused the nation, declared war, and sent us into World War II kicking butts left and right. BOOM! YEAH, AMERICA!

To prepare for your inevitable moment like this, you should go over the following sample crises that could possibly befall our great country. With each, you'll find some of the departments and groups that handle it and the steps with which you can implement a plan. Oh, and just assume each of these scenarios involve Congress. You're probably going to need funding and stuff and that can only be approved by passing some legislation. I mean, you could do it via an executive order, but that's not the best method.

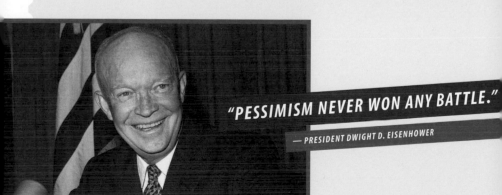

"PESSIMISM NEVER WON ANY BATTLE."

— PRESIDENT DWIGHT D. EISENHOWER

SAMPLE CRISIS: NATURAL DISASTER

WHO CAN HELP:
★ Federal Emergency Management Agency (FEMA)
★ Local Rescue Agencies
★ National Guard

WHO CAN'T HELP:
★ Food & Drug Administration (FDA)
★ Immigration & Customs Enforcement (ICE)
★ Bureau of Alcohol, Tobacco, Firearms, & Explosives (ATF)

WHAT TO DO:
★ Send in FEMA
★ Work with local officials
★ Secure needed funding for relief and reconstruction

WHAT NOT TO DO:
★ Send in Dwayne "The Rock" Johnson. (He's just an actor.)
★ Tour devastation for photo op
★ Offer only thoughts and prayers

SAMPLE CRISIS: ALIEN INVASION

WHO CAN HELP:
- ★ Department of Defense
- ★ National Security Administration
- ★ Department of Homeland Security
- ★ National Aeronautics & Space Administration (NASA)

WHO CAN'T HELP:
- ★ Federal Bureau of Investigation (FBI)
- ★ Bureau of Engraving & Printing (BEP)
- ★ Department of Commerce

WHAT TO DO:
- ★ Hunker down in the Situation Room
- ★ Send in the military
- ★ Hope the aliens favor your side of the aisle

WHAT NOT TO DO:
- ★ Drop a nuke on a populated area
- ★ Ignore scientific data
- ★ Make Roland Emmerich the Secretary of Defense

SAMPLE CRISIS: ESCALATING TENSION BETWEEN NATIONS

WHO CAN HELP:
- ★ State Department
- ★ Joint Chiefs of Staff
- ★ Department of Defense (DoD)

WHO CAN'T HELP:
- ★ Department of Labor (DoL)
- ★ Department of Health & Human Services(HHS)
- ★ National Fish & Wildlife Foundation (NFWF)

WHAT TO DO:
- ★ Gather information from State Department
- ★ Listen to advice and options from Joint Chiefs
- ★ Prepare DoD for contingencies

WHAT NOT TO DO:
- ★ Escalate tensions with confrontational language
- ★ Circumvent established diplomatic channels
- ★ Say the phrase "I dare you"

EPILOGUE

So, that's everything. So, I hope you've learned that the United States of America is a wonderful place because, truly, anyone can be president. I also hope you've learned that it takes WAY more than just those three simple requirements laid out by our founding fathers to actually be president.

You need a basic, grade-level, working knowledge of how to campaign and how to govern. If you don't have these, your campaign and (hopefully, single) presidential term will be a total hot mess and three-ring circus. Plus, you may shine an unnecessary spotlight on the fragile democratic framework on which this country is founded, one that might leave our great nation open to ridicule and scorn, thus unseating us from the position of the world's most only superpower. But, let's not go there.

It doesn't matter if you are conservative or liberal, male or female, gay or straight (or somewhere in between or beyond), if you are a citizen of this great nation, you can be president. And if you have no designs on sitting behind that big ol' desk in the Oval Office, that's OK. Because the important thing to remember, something you read earlier in this book: there is one person in this country who has more power than the president… No, not Congress… I mean, they have equal power, and that's more than one person… No, I mean the American citizen.

That American ideal, that American dream—it's a real thing. So, even if after reading this you are still not inspired to run for the highest office in the land, the great news is you can still get involved in our democratic process and the process of governing. You can vote, you can volunteer, you can share your thoughts and concerns with your fellow voters, your representatives in Congress, and, yes, your president. They work for you, after all.

But if you do decide to run, if you want to go for the big gig, we'd be happy to have you in the mix. And, hey, being the President of the United States is a pretty awesome job. Everything after that is just gravy. Like, what are you going to do after that, build a rocket? So, what? You were already president, you show-off.

YOU ARE PRESIDENT!

VICTORY IS YOURS. GAME ON.

It's time to put everything you've learned in this book to the test with a choose-your-own presidential adventure story. How will you fare as president? Find out when you are presented with a massive national crisis and options at each step on how to proceed. The cool thing is that here—unlike IRL— if you screw up, you can go always back to the beginning, pick a different path, and be a better decider! Or not.

Your hand trembles with excitement and joy as you raise it. Your other hand rests firmly on the Bible. This is it, the moment you for which you fought and prepared. The judge swearing you in says words and you repeat them, but your head buzzes with disbelief. You did it. You are president!

The inauguration crowd, which stretches out as far as you can see, cheers as you are officially sworn into office. But the joyful mood of the moment turns silent when the mid-morning sky darkens. You look skyward and see a huge oval shadow passing overhead. The object rumbles high above the winter clouds. Someone in the crowd screams. The piercing sound snaps the attendees out of their trance and they scatter, tripping over each other in fear.

You feel two arms wrap around you. It's Agent Islay, the head of your new Secret Service detail. He and the other agents rush you off the stage and through a series of rooms and halls. Then you burst out of a door and into a waiting limousine. Islay climbs in next to you, and the driver slams his foot on the gas. The car leaves a long batch of black rubber as it tears out onto the road.

"What in the son of a monkey is happening?!" you ask Islay.

He holds his finger to his earpiece, trying to hear the information coming through. "Yes," he says into the mic hidden in his shirt cuff. "We have the president." He turns to you and says a sentence you never thought you'd ever hear. "Mr./Madam President, it appears an alien fleet of approximately 300 ships is hovering above the continental United States."

You lean over and look out the window. You see the massive craft slowly making its way across the sky above D.C. "My God," you say as a little bit of pee escapes your private bit.

Islay says, "Both the Joint Chiefs of Staff and the House Intelligence Committee are available. With whom would you like to meet?"

If you want to meet with the **Joint Chiefs of Staff**, turn to page 5.
If you want to meet with the **House Intelligence Committee**, turn to page 14.

With efficiency only the activated U.S. military can provide, massive lights and landing markers are placed in the Bonneville Salt Flats in northwestern Utah. From the safety of the Situation Room, you monitor the activity as hundreds of tanks, cannons, and soldiers form a miles-long circle around the landing area. You give the go sign, which is relayed by phone to the commanding officer. On the screen moments later, you see an array of powerful spotlights flicker on and swirl around the base of a nearby craft methodically floating west.

To the surprise of everyone, the ship begins to lower from the sky. It lumbers downward toward the landing area. Soldiers around the perimeter point their rifles at the craft as it stops fifty feet above the ground. The ship goes quiet. It just sits there, hanging in the air.

Then there's a huge metallic squeak, and a red beam bursts from the belly of the craft. It makes a circle, washing over the soldiers, tanks, and other equipment. However, it appears to do no harm.

The commanding officer picks up his walkie-talkie, which is piped directly into the Situation Room, and shouts, "Mr./Madam President, that thing seems to be scanning us! We should open fire now!"

A science advisor standing next to you leans over and says, "Sir/Madam, we should go with the plan. They don't want to land here. Let's attempt to make contact and proceed from there."

Your Chief of Staff leans over and whispers in your ear, which makes you jump because you didn't even know he was there. He quietly says, "Let's see how this plays out."

If you agree with the commanding officer, turn to page 6.
If you agree with your science advisor, turn to page 10.
If you agree with your Chief of Staff, turn to page 16.

You are immediately put in touch with a team of military and civilian advisors, the necessary first step before issuing the launch order. You discuss the situation and all agree to go ahead and initiate a nuclear strike on the alien fleet. You officially give the command. This scenario has been tested for decades but never implemented until now. It goes flawlessly and within minutes the order makes its way to the launch crews.

Simultaneously, across the entire country and from submarines stationed in the Pacific, Atlantic, and the Gulf, large missiles burst from their silos and rise. In cities and rural town all across the country, citizens watch as the rockets leave white trails that cut through the peaceful blue sky. The nuclear missiles reach our uppermost stratosphere where the alien fleet hovers. Then a rapid series of brilliant, blinding flashes bleach out the sky. Seconds later, a succession of thunderous claps disturbs the nationwide silence. Millions of pieces of alien craft rain down, burning as the fall, creating a stunning meteor shower-like show. All across the country, people cheer. The alien fleet is destroyed.

The sky begins to darken and the temperature drops. By the end of the afternoon, even people who live in warm southern states witness their local waterways freezing. In the northern states, the situation is much worse. Reports come in from Mexico and Canada of similarly extreme weather.

In the comfort of the Situation Room, the monitors are full of images of a dark world covered in frost and ice. You turn to an advisor and ask, "What is happening?"

The advisor looks at the monitors and says, "The explosions have blocked out the sun. We never thought it would actually happen, but we appear to have entered what theorists call a nuclear winter."

"How long will it last?" you ask.

The advisor turns to you and says, "Forever."

With horror, you realize you've just started a new ice age and doomed the people of the entire planet to a slow icy death. And it's only your first day as president.

THE END

It's strange how you dreamed of the moment you'd first enter the Oval Office and take a seat behind the big desk. Now you're finally here, but there's no time to sit. You and a few key advisors stand around the desk, staring at the speakerphone. On the line is Dr. Vance Osteen, director of NASA.

"Well, Sir/Madam," Osteen says, "From what we've been able to observe, there don't appear to be any weaponry with which we're familiar. And judging from the shape of the ship, we feel these are exploratory vessels."

You shrug your shoulders and say, "So, these aliens just flew all the way across the galaxy to make like an intergalactic Lewis and Clark." You lean on the desk and quietly ask, "What if they're here to colonize, like…Christopher Columbus?"

"There is that possibility, Sir/Madam," he says. "But we still suggest we try to make contact."

Roger Dougal, your Chief of Staff, shakes his head and says, "We should contain this. Let's find an area away from civilization to create a landing area for them and surround it with a substantial military presence."

If you agree with NASA, turn to page 10.
If you agree with your Chief of Staff, turn to page 2.

Forget the orientation tour. Islay leads you quickly through the White House, down a few hallways and a flight of stairs. There, you're confronted with two huge doors. Islay gestures to a handprint scanner on the wall. You place your hand on the glass and the doors swing open. Islay says, "Welcome to the Situation Room, Mr./Madam President."

Inside you find the Chief of Staff of the Army, the Commandant of the Marine Corps, the Chief of the Navy, and the Chief of Staff of the Air Force, as well as a few other advisors, seated around a huge table. The walls are lined with monitors, each showing hulking alien ships silently hovering above cities all across the U.S.

Everyone stands as you enter and you gesture for them to sit. You ask, "What do we know?"

Army General Dwayne Samson glances around the room, then says, "Not much, Sir/Madam." He slides you a file full of photos and other data. "They weren't detected until moments ago, which leads us to believe they have some sort of cloaking technology. That plus the sheer scientific feat of build-ing a fleet of crafts that can travel through space means they probably have advanced weaponry as well."

You close the file. "Do we have any idea why they're here?"

"No, Sir/Madam," Samson says. "And to be perfectly honest, there's some dis-agreement among us on exactly what to do next. The commandant and I be-lieve the lack of any attempt at communication from the ships means they are in the early stages of a nationwide attack So we should launch a preemptive strike before they're able to coordinate their offensive." He gestures to the representatives from the Navy and Air Force "However, they feel we should bring in some scientists and theorists to come up with an alternative...less aggressive plan. What would you like to do?"

If you would like to launch an attack on the alien fleet, turn to page 3.
If you would like to hear from scientists and theorists, turn to page 9.

You push your advisor out of the way and issue the command, "Open fire."

On the monitors, you see muzzle flashes from all around the perimeter as the soldiers shoot their rifles and machine guns. Tanks launch huge missiles. Explosions and shouts fill the air around the ship. It seems to go on for hours, but in reality, it only lasts for a few minutes before the commander shouts, "Cease fire!"

The desert wind blows the smoke away to reveal an amazing sight. The ship and the alien are untouched, unscathed.

A metallic voice emanates from the ship and fills the air. It bellows, "We are having trouble understanding your intensions. We ask you, do you wish to welcome us?"

The commander's voice, stern and steady, comes over the speaker in the Situation Room. He says, "That ship isn't even scratched. I say we wait for this one to rejoin the fleet and then launch the nukes, Sir/Madam. That'll wipe 'em out clean."

If you would like to welcome the aliens, turn to page 11.
If you want to launch nuclear missiles, turn to page 3.

With the help of the FBI, your Deputy of Communications tracks down a phone number of Carl Hastings, the CEO of MUFON, The Mutual U.F.O. Network. You and a few key White House staff members dial the number and turn on the speaker. Hastings picks up and, through a mouth full of potato chips, says, "Kinda busy right now."

You say, "Mr. Hastings. This is the president."

"President of what?" he asks, still munching.

You answer, "The United States."

You hear the phone clunk against something as if it were dropped. After a second or two, Hastings returns and says, "How can I help you, Sir/Madam?"

You explain that the House Intelligence Committee suggested his organization offer a suggestion on how to handle this latest development. Hastings's breathing increases. Like you felt earlier at the inauguration, he's been waiting his whole life for this moment.

"At our last panel discussion about this scenario, the conclusions we reached were that these beings would either come to reclaim materials and tech held at Area 51, so we should make that available to them, or that they would arrive as diplomats and, as a gesture of our willingness to work with them, we should give them Iowa."

"Why Iowa?" you ask.

Hastings says, "Because it's possible most of the population of that state are already space aliens."

If you want to open up Area 51 to the aliens, turn to page 11.
If you want to offer the aliens Iowa, turn to page 8.

It takes quite a bit of convincing, but the Governor of Iowa finally agrees to welcome the aliens, should they choose to stay. You give the go ahead for the signal to be sent to the alien fleet: PLEASE, JOIN US. YOU CAN HAVE IOWA.

Almost immediately, the ships begin to align over Iowa, creating a massive hovering tower. A small envoy of aliens, which look like slithering bluish octopuses, arrives in Des Moines and are welcomed by the governor, representatives from the State Senate, and members of a local Boy Scout troop. It makes a fantastic photo op.

Soon all of the aliens start arriving in small transports. The local government offices are flooded with extraterrestrials seeking tourist maps and "bleeglars," whatever those are. Things descend into chaos.

After a few hours it becomes clear that something drastic needs to happen. You consult your Chief of Staff, who presents polling data that shows citizens of the remaining forty-nine states think Iowa needs federal assistance to help assimilate all of the new residents. Your National Security Advisor says his research shows the best plan is to completely enclose Iowa with a giant wall and let the aliens figure things out for themselves.

If you decide to go with your Chief of Staff's polling data, turn to page 12.
If you decide to go with your National Security Advisor's plan, turn to page 13.

A team of scientists and theorists are ushered into a large conference room in the White House. You haven't seen so many nerds since your sister dragged you to that LARPer convention.

"You've been apprised of the situation," you say. "So, what do you, the greatest minds humanity has to offer, think we should do?"

Warren Söderström, theoretical astrophysicist and bass player, says, "We feel like there is no reason to believe these beings traveled across the galaxy to destroy us. We believe you should take a page out of the Voyager playbook and attempt to make contact via a series of audio recordings, like people saying 'hello' in different languages, maybe some Rolling Stones—"

"Of course, Stephen Hawking disagreed," interrupts Joint Chief General Samson. "He believed that any alien species would see us as inferior, so if they ever arrived at our doorstep, it could only be to destroy us. I strongly urge you to launch the attack we suggested."

Söderström sheepishly raises his hand. You gesture to him and say, "Yes?"

He stammers, "I…I skipped lunch. Do you have any Hot Pockets?"

If you decide to listen to the scientists, turn to page 10.
If you decide to listen to the Joint Chief, turn to page 3.

Your advisors put you in touch with Susan Chang, multibillionaire CEO and creator of Z-Space, a private company that developed low-cost rocket technology now used by NASA and other agencies to deliver personnel and payloads to space. The company also makes fantastic blenders.

"If you want to make contact," she says, "I can get you to them. We have a new rocket. It's called Ice Dragon Omega."

You reply, "Oooooh, that's a cool name."

"Yes," she says. "That's why we picked it. It can deliver a light payload, like a crew and supplies. We can easily and quickly equip it with a large video screen so we can show messages or images to the alien crafts."

"Great! How long will all that take?" you ask.

She says, "It's ready now. I had my team do it while we were talking."

"That's amazing!"

"I know," she quips. "It's like some sort of fictional story or something."

Two hours later, Ice Dragon Omega lifts off from the Z-Space International Center on one of Chang's private islands. Onboard are two Z-Space pilots and two representatives from your new, hastily formed Department of Inter-galactic Affairs. The rocket sails up into the mesosphere to meet the alien crafts. Once near one of the ships, Ice Dragon Omega goes into hover mode. The massive video screen lights up with the message agreed upon by your team of military and science advisors. It says: S'UP?

An entire side of the closest craft lights up as if constructed by billions of tiny bulbs. Colors swirl on the huge screen and form the words: NOT MUCH. S'UP WITH YOU?

Communication with an alien race has been established. The next step could define your entire presidency. Your team of science advisors suggests you welcome them and your military advisors suggest you turn them away.

If you agree with your science advisors, turn to page 8.
If you agree with your military advisors, turn to page 15.

The Director of the FBI disagrees with you, but you insist this is the right way to go. You issue an executive order to immediately open the military installation known as Area 51 and welcome the aliens. Search lights are installed around the facility and as the sun sets, the evening sky is painted with swirling beams, letting the visitors know they may land.

Through the course of the night, the ships align over the base in a tall hovering tower that stretches into the stratosphere. Smaller crafts transport the tentacled creatures to the base, where they are greeted by Army General Louise Howard and a team of representatives from the military and science community. The aliens wave their slimy arms as they are shown the wreckage of one of their ships from decades ago. The scientists quickly determine waving their appendages means they are happy.

Days pass and the days stretch into week, then months. By spring, Area 51 has become a thriving community of aliens and humans working together to advance our technology and educate the unearthly residents about our own culture.

Ten years later, after your two stellar presidential terms have ended, you are invited to the ribbon cutting of the opulent Area 51 Hotel and Casino, a joint venture between the aliens and the military. The revenue from the popular attraction goes to fund local and federal programs and helps drastically reduce our financial dependence on taxes and trade.

You go down in history as the first intergalactic diplomat. Two decades after your death, the Galactic Alliance unanimously approves a universe-wide holiday in your honor, and your face graces the spleewok, a form of currency widely used throughout the Milky Way and beyond.

THE END

For once, Congress acts quickly to pass a law allowing federal funding for the newly named Iowa Intergalactic Zone (IIZ). You happily sign it, and it doesn't take long before social workers, biologists, administrators, and others flood the state.

Centers are set up to assist the new residents with housing and other necessities, classes are offered to teach them about our culture and allow them to teach us about theirs, job training and placement services help the strange beings enter the workforce and grow the local economy, medical and biological experts become familiar with the creatures' unique physiology and set up facilities to offer emergency and non-emergency care.

As time passes, the IIZ grows into a popular tourist destination for people from all over the world. And with the help of the new citizens, innovation thrives, solidifying America's place as the world's technology leader. Advancements and inventions include the Zippy Pippy, a low-cost flying car that runs on good conversation, and the Boopleblort, which turns literally anything into a nice cappuccino.

You kick off your second presidential term with the unveiling of a new passport, which allows the aliens to travel beyond the borders of the IIZ. And the federal funding allows the creation of the Human and Alien Education Act, which makes college affordable for all, no matter their planet of birth.

After graduating from Harvard, an alien named Kleeeenar Vixlpqsoewie (aka Kevin) goes on to become the country's first alien senator, representing the IIZ in Washington D.C. He later sponsors a popular bill (that eventually becomes law) he names after you that makes education free for everyone.

THE END

For once, Congress acts quickly to pass a law allowing federal funding to build a wall around the entire state of Iowa. Construction costs billions and takes years. To pay for it all, you call for a cut in budgets across the board—education, military, infrastructure, and other programs are drastically defunded.

As the project goes on, the lack of adequate funding for alien assimilation causes the entire state to descend into chaos. Aliens are housed in dilapidated housing projects and human residents begin to resent being cut off from the rest of the country. Tensions start to rise.

As the wall nears completion, violent clashes occur between a newly unified group of creatures and humans in Iowa and the skeletal but heavily armed military presence sent to keep them in line. Following a series of daring raids by the self-called Mixed Iowa Liberation Force (MILF), the military in the state is overthrown and the aliens are able to reclaim their ships.

You issue a command to send in more military to restore order, but thanks to your budget cuts, the mission titled Destabilize Iowa's Liberation Force (DILF) fails miserably. The MILF captures multiple shipments of weapons and explosives. Then, on a day that comes to be known as Liberation Day, the wall is systematically blown up. That act signals the beginning of America's second Civil War.

The aliens and a huge contingent of humans wage war. The country divides in half with the western states fighting alongside the creatures against the eastern states. Thanks to the aliens' advanced technology, the war goes down in history as the bloodiest and most deadly in American history, especially when we learned when the aliens win a battle, they eat the surviving members of the opposing side. The battle cry, "No prisoners! Only lunch!" spreads and soon the human members of the western army adopt the tradition. The alien/cannibal army decimates the eastern army.

The last city to fall is Washington D.C. As flames fill the sky, the victors march into White House. You crouch behind your desk in the Oval Office. Alien General Furfnurgle and Admiral Jones kick in the door. The General looks at you and says, "Nice to eat you, Mr./Madam President."

THE END

Islay ushers you into a massive meeting room within the White House. Seated and standing around a huge table are the numerable members of the House Permanent Select Committee on Intelligence, which works with and oversees all of the intelligence-gathering entities within the government and beyond.

As you enter, people stand. You gesture for them to sit. Someone offers you a chair, but you wave off the gesture. There's no time to get comfortable. "What have you found out?" you ask.

Representative Jennifer Washington, the committee chairwoman, says, "We know they are definitely not another nation's experimental craft, the ships are able to go undetected by any know method of tracking, they're made of an unknown element that makes it impossible to scan, and whatever is piloting those ships has made scientific advances well beyond our own."

"Yeah, I figured all that out on the car ride here," you say. "You are in charge of gathering information. What can we find out?"

Washington glances around the room, then says, "We need another source, a source with which we typically don't work."

"Like what?" you ask.

Washington says, "NASA, who'll be able to shine some light on the ships themselves."

Belinda Miles, your Director of Communications, says, "We should call MUFON, the Mutual U.F.O. Network."

"Those crackpots?!" you exclaim.

Miles nods. "Until now, I thought so too. But they have decades of research on this topic and can speak to possible alien behavior."

If you agree with the House Permanent Select Committee on Intelligence, turn to page 4.
If you agree with your Director of Communications, turn to page 7.

You issue the order to display the next message: YOU ARE NOT WELCOME. PLEASE LEAVE. All of civilization waits and watches on televisions and computer screens to see what happens next.

After what seems like hours, colors swirl on the side of the alien craft once again. They form letters that read: WE CONSIDER SUCH WORDS AN INSULT. PREPARE TO BE ENSLAVED.

A red beam emanates from the side of the craft and strikes Ice Dragon Omega. The rocket explodes killing all onboard. The entire alien fleet lowers through the stratosphere and, in a simultaneous and coordinated attack, they fire beams on any populated area they encounter. Millions die as population centers are leveled. The horizon glows with the fire of hundreds of destroyed cities. Hades has risen!

Some surviving humans make it to the wilderness to hide, but most are rounded up by the aliens. These enslaved humans are each fitted with a collar and a corresponding tag. Individuals are assigned to alien families where they eat from containers placed on the floor.

As you are fitted with a collar and led to one of the creature's quarters, you realize with horror what is happening. Because of your actions, what's left of the population of the United States have been turned into house pets. And it's only your first day as president.

THE END

You agree with your Chief of Staff. After all, this is a huge moment for your presidency and you'd hate to be the guy who got all trigger happy or told everyone to leave just when it appeared we're about to make contact.

The craft hangs in the air about the Salt Flats for ten minutes, then thirty minutes, then an hour. A few of the soldiers around the perimeter fall asleep. After three hours, the craft lets out a piercing hiss and a gangway unfolds from the belly of the structure.

Down the ramp, comes a tall creature with bluish green skin and what appear to be clusters of tentacles extending from its torso. It looks like it just slithered out of a nightmare or a really, really bad blind date. From an unseen loudspeaker somewhere on the ship, a voice bellows, "We have been waiting for an official welcome for quite some time… Are we just going to sit here all day? Because, I mean, we have stuff to do."

In the Situation Room, you scramble for the receiver, which is patched directly into the public-address system at the landing site. You clear your throat. This is it, humanity's first contact with an alien life-form. You must choose your words carefully. You clear your throat again. Your mouth feels dry. On the table in front of you is a can of soda. You consider taking a drink to wet your whistle a bit before speaking.

If you take a drink to wet your mouth before speaking, turn to page 17.
If you soldier on and speak with a dry mouth, turn to page 18.

You take a huge pull from the soda. The tickle in your throat disappears and you raise the receiver. You open your mouth to utter the first words any human will say to an extraterrestrial life.

A guttural belch escapes your stomach and erupts from your throat. People in the room gasp. On the monitors, you hear your thunderous burp blast from the public-address system at the Salt Flats. This is not how you expected to go down in history.

The alien does not respond. Another hiss escapes the ship and the gangway begins to raise again. The ship lifts into the air, joining the others floating above the country. On televisions, computers, and mobile devices, hundreds of millions of citizens wait to see what happens next.

Emanating from the ships, a message is broadcast to the entire population of the United States at one time. The single booming alien voice says, "There is no civilized life here. We shall continue on, searching for a planet with which to share our vast riches and technological innovations. Goodbye, primitive beings."

As if controlled by a single mind, the crafts lift higher into the stratosphere and beyond. They fly off into deep space in search of some other planet, some other life.

You only last one term as president. For the rest of your life, you are known as the person who belched away humanity's greatest advancement.

THE END

There's no time for refreshments. You mentally review the line you prepared for just such an encounter: "America welcomes you, visitors, to our marvelous planet."

You raise the receiver and, with a dry mouth, say, "Amurikah, wecombs ooo, fishiters…" Your garbled words are broadcast through the public-address system at the Salt Flats. You think, "Uh-oh."

From the craft, a booming alien voice replies, "Fooosh yaaalllipeee nuthall!"

The creature on the gangway is joined by a few more, then tens more, then hundreds. They all descend the gangway. On the monitor, you watch as one with shimmering green suction cups (presumably their leader) approaches the commanding officer. You hear the alien being say to him, "Thank you for such a warm invitation, and in our own language. We will happily take you up on your offer."

The commanding officer says, "What off—" but his words are cut off when the creature opens its mouth and swallows the military man whole. Other aliens slither around the perimeter and swallow soldiers.

Gunfire erupts at the scene. The person operating the video feed for the Situation Room is either eaten or runs away, knocking over the camera. Your view in the Situation Room turns sideways with a crash. The sound of screams and explosions fill the room.

You've accidentally invited an alien race to eat us, starting an intergalactic war. And it's only your first day as president.

THE END

ABOUT THE AUTHOR

[YOUR FACE HERE]

Former journalist David Vienna was raised by a newspaper editor and a lobbyist in the D.C. area. The only election he ever won was the "Best Sense of Humor" superlative during his senior year of high school, though it is rumored that there was Russian meddling. He is also the author of *Are We There Yet?*, *Drinks for Mundane Tasks*, and the bestselling parenting manifesto *Calm The F*ck Down*. He is the president of his own fan club.

ACKNOWLEDGEMENTS

Thanks to my mom, dad, and stepmom, who taught me more about politics than any class, book, or pundit ever could.

Re-elect
[your
name here].